Christian
Morality
& You

Revised Edition

Christian

Morality

& You

Right and Wrong
In an Age of Freedom

MICHAEL PENNOCK with James Finley

Ave Maria Press   Notre Dame, Indiana

Nihil Obstat:
> Rev. Mark DiNardo
> *Censor Deputatus*

Imprimatur:
> Most Rev. James A. Hickey, S.T.D.
> *Bishop of Cleveland*

© 1984 Ave Maria Press, Notre Dame, Indiana

Library of Congress Catalog Card Number: 83-73085
International Standard Book Number: 0-87793-308-1

Photography:
> Hildegard Adler, 46; Marne Breckensiek, 34; Ron Byers, 24; Ed Carlin, 13; Alan Cliburn, 137; Roger A. Davison, 54; John E. Fitzgerald, 65; Franciscan Friars of Marytown, 164; Genesis Project, Inc., 50; Luke Golobitsh, 112; Jack Hamilton, 173; Ia.-Kan., 73; H. T. Kellner, front cover; Wm. Koechling, 144; David J. McConnell, 101; Carolyn McKeone, 131, 136; R. Meier, 154; Joanne Meldrum, 41, 76; Ron Meyer, back cover; Jonathan A. Meyers, 92; Roger Neal, 19; Panographics, 63; Gene Plaisted, 8, 170, 186; Will & Angie Rumpf, 30; Paul M. Schrock, 58; Vernon Sigl, 27; Bob Taylor, 82, 106, 118; UNICEF photo by David Robinson, 124.

Manufactured in the United States of America.

DEDICATION

We dedicate this revised edition to all of our students—
past, present and future. May the Lord shower them
with his many blessings and call them to do
great things for his kingdom.

Acknowledgments

We'd like to thank here once again all those individuals who helped us with the first edition of this book: Monsignor William Novicky, Father Mark DiNardo, Father Dennis Dillon, S.J., Father Paul Hritz, Sister Mary Owen, S.N.D., Sister Mary Andre, O.S.U., Father Don Cozzens, Sister Mary Cathy Hilkert, O.P., Sister Carolyn Capuano, H.M., Sister Ruth Ann Bruner, H.M., Sister Pat Kozak, C.S.J., Sister Patricia Finn, C.S.J., Sister Marian Durkin, C.S.A., Dr. Frederick Schnell, Steve Schnell, Patrick Riley, Rosey Torrence, Blair Chirdon, Bert Polito, Sister Mary Borgias, S.N.D., Sister Julie Marie, S.N.D. and the theology faculty of St. Ignatius High School. Their prayers, critical advice, encouragement and confidence in us helped launch this high school series for Ave Maria Press.

We'd also like to thank our wives—Kaye Finley and Carol Pennock—for their continued moral support and abiding love.

In a special way, too, we'd like to thank all of our students who have responded to our teaching. May the Lord bless them and help them live as his presence in the world.

Special thanks to Bob Previts for his many helpful ideas for this revised edition.

And, finally, we wish to acknowledge how grateful we are to be associated with Ave Maria Press and the many wonderful people there who have helped us: Gene Geissler who was our first editor, Frank Cunningham, Joan Bellina, Charlie Jones and Father John Reedy.

Contents

ONE

Who Are You?

Each of us is an epitome of the world, each a little world in ourself, in which all that is to be found in the great world of the universe is to be found.
—St. Francis de Sales

Why begin a book on Christian morality with a chapter entitled "Who Are You?" After all, don't most of us know who we are? What has the question of our identity to do with what is right and what is wrong?

A real help in defining and describing who we are comes from looking at ourselves in relationship to others. And, in turn, it is in knowing ourselves that we better understand how we ought to act toward others.

Before we discuss the issue of who we are, let us see how you would answer the question right now. Below you will find seven brief descriptions of the human person as seen by various philosophies. These descriptions are simplified and contain just a kernel thought which helps us to characterize a particular way of looking at who we are.

WHO ARE YOU?

Under each description is a numbering system which asks whether you strongly agree (5), agree somewhat (4), are indifferent to (3), disagree somewhat (2), or strongly disagree (1) with the statements made.

9

Philosophy #1: "I cannot live locked up inside myself. I must be open to the world and those around me. Yet I must be meditative so that I can overcome all illusion about myself and the world and thus discover ultimate reality."

☐	☐	☐	☐	☐
5	4	3	2	1

Philosophy #2: "I'm here for one purpose: to get as much out of life as I can. Pain and suffering are evils that must be avoided at all costs. The main thing in life is to feel good."

☐	☐	☐	☐	☐
5	4	3	2	1

Philosophy #3: "My value depends on my work for the good of the group. 'From each according to ability; to each according to need' is a good motto for society. Individual rights must always be subordinated to the goals of the group."

☐	☐	☐	☐	☐
5	4	3	2	1

Philosophy #4: "I must do whatever I can to guarantee my freedom to do what I want to do. Good is that which furthers my interests."

☐	☐	☐	☐	☐
5	4	3	2	1

Philosophy #5: "I have value. I strive to live a full life of loving service for other people, all of whom are my brothers and sisters. Life has a final meaning which resides outside of me, that is, in God and in my relationship to Jesus Christ."

☐	☐	☐	☐	☐
5	4	3	2	1

Philosophy #6: "In the light of death, life has no real meaning. It is a joke, 'the tale of an idiot signifying nothing.' "

☐	☐	☐	☐	☐
5	4	3	2	1

Philosophy #7: "I believe in order and well-being for everyone. I try to treat other people the way I would want to be treated. I try to be a good person. I don't think about God or religion much; they don't make a real difference in the way I live my life."

☐	☐	☐	☐	☐
5	4	3	2	1

These simplified versions of how some people view who we are illustrate contrasting outlooks on life; they depict various ways of searching for meaning. We will discuss several of these in more detail later in the chapter. Briefly, however, the major views the above descriptions represent are the following:

Philosophy #1 describes an *Oriental* view. Some Buddhists, for example, try to live a life of gentle submissiveness to the cosmic powers flowing in the universe, powers which they try to let control their destiny.

Philosophy #2 corresponds to the *Playboy* theory of life (sometimes known as *hedonism*). Pleasure, especially physical pleasure, is almost made into a god. You will find this philosophy in many of the advertisements bombarding the American scene today.

Philosophy #3 delineates a *communistic* view of the human person. The best-known exponent of this way of life is 19th-century political economist and philosopher Karl Marx, who preached that people have worth only to the degree that they help the interests of the state. Over half of the world's population is dominated by this view of humanity.

Philosophy #4 depicts an extremely individualistic way of looking at people. It is sometimes called *atheistic existentialism,* and its most famous proponent was the French writer Jean-Paul Sartre. Sartre believed that each person is radically alone and separated from all others.

Philosophy #5 describes a *Christian* way of life. Chapter 2 will develop in some detail the presuppositions of this view.

Philosophy #6 corresponds to a *nihilistic* world view which maintains that our lives have no ultimate meaning. This philosophy was especially popular in Europe during the aftermath of the Great Depression.

Finally, Philosophy #7 represents *secular humanism,* a philosophy of life that concerns itself with the achievements and interests of human beings. It does not address questions about God or religion at all. So many people live by this philosophy that the Fathers of Vatican II felt compelled to mention how pervasive its views have become:

> In numerous places these views are voiced not only in the teachings of philosophers, but on every side they influence literature, the arts, the interpretation of the humanities and of history, and civil laws themselves (*Pastoral Constitution on the Church in the Modern World,* No. 7).

THE IMPORTANCE OF OUR CONCEPT OF THE HUMAN PERSON

The exercise at the beginning of the chapter helped us think about ourselves and about others. This is important to do because our behavior toward others often enough flows from what we think the human person is. Even our attitudes toward others are affected by the way we think about humanity. The theory we consciously or unconsciously hold about others strikingly determines our practice toward them.

A couple of examples may help here. Have you ever met a person for the first time and immediately liked him or her? Do you remember how you acted? You were probably kind, considerate and well-disposed toward the person. Or is there somebody you don't like even though you can't understand why? You might find yourself being rude and short-tempered for no apparent reason. Perhaps it's because the person gave you a negative impression the first time you met. This negative impression stays with you and affects your subsequent attitudes to the person.

The first example brings to mind a famous psychological experiment in the education field. The purpose of the experiment was to test the theory that our general idea of people strongly affects our behavior toward them. In the experiment a group of teachers was told that a new class of students was a "superior" group. In reality the class was quite average in ability. But because the students were labeled "bright," the teachers expected good results. In fact, the class *did* perform as a superior group. The teachers' positive attitudes toward the students helped them to above-average levels of achievement.

One thing is sure: We all have a philosophy of what a human person is or should be. We are brought up in an environment which works on certain assumptions about who people are. We naturally, and very often unconsciously, absorb these assumptions and theories without ever examining them critically to see how valid they are. Advertising, sports, movies, television, business and numerous other social pressures greatly affect the way we view a person and consequently how we should act.

For example, look at modern advertisements. Commercials for deodorants, mouthwashes, skin-blemish removers and other cosmetics all operate on the basic assumption that we are creatures who must be *physically* attractive to have much worth in the eyes of others. These ads try to sell the American public the following concept of the person: To have good breath and white teeth is to be a good and worthwhile person; to have bad breath is to be socially undesirable and worthless.

Note how this view can affect us in our relationships to others. Aren't we tempted to look at the externals which people present to us—their looks, perhaps, or their possessions—rather than who they are as people? The "beautiful people" are not really better than the rest of us, and probably not worse either. But notice how advertisements and movies present them as ideal people for us to imitate and look up to.

Advertisements also entice us with the catchy little ditties that say, "You owe it to yourself." Sophisticated ads and commercials sell us on *consumerism.* Consumerism encourages buying even if we cannot afford the product and even if we don't need it. The real dehumanizing effect of consumerism is that it takes place at the expense of others. We Americans consume nonessential items while the poor of the world get poorer and poorer. It is not that our commercialized society tells us not to think about the poor; rather, it sells us on our need to indulge *ourselves.* But it is in indulging ourselves that we often forget others.

DISCUSSION

1. In what way has advertising influenced you to buy something in recent months? What are some of the assumptions about the human person which are behind these advertisements?

2. Can you think of other influences in modern society that push a certain view of the human person? Why do you think people accept these influences so easily?

EXERCISE

Reflecting on the following questions might help you decide what is a worthwhile view of human beings. Circle Y—Yes, I agree with this statement; N—No, I disagree with this statement; or ?—I don't know where I stand on this question.

I think that . . .

1. rapists should be executed . . . . Y N ?

2. politicians are generally honest . . . . Y N ?

3. honesty is the best policy . . . . Y N ?

4. the arms race is a major sign that humanity is sick . . Y N ?

5. the poor are generally lazy . . . . Y N ?

6. the women's rights issues are getting a little
   tiresome . . . . Y N ?

7. people are essentially greedy . . . . Y N ?

8. people are too easily led and don't think for
   themselves . . . . Y N ?

9. people usually want to do the right thing . . . . Y N ?

10. the world is too pleasure-oriented today . . . . Y N ?

- Share your responses with your classmates.
- What do your answers reflect about your philosophy of the human person?
- Choose one of the following:

    ____a. People are basically good.

    ____b. People are basically evil.

DIFFERENT PHILOSOPHIES AND
HOW ONE SHOULD ACT

As we have discussed in the previous section, it is rather easy to see that our view of what it means to be a person greatly affects the way we act toward others. Consider again the example of hedonism. This *"Playboy* philosophy" views others as objects whose purpose in life is merely to provide pleasure. In relating to others the hedonist will tend to avoid total commitment to the other because it might involve sacrifice or pain, and sacrifice and pain lessen pleasure. Thus a total commitment like marriage is taboo for the *Playboy* type. Marriage, for hedonists, is all right only as long as it is convenient and comfortable.

The Marxian-communist view affects many people in today's world. In this philosophy the individual is subordinated to the group. Individual rights, therefore, exist only by the whim of the state. The right to worship, to work where one pleases, to speak out freely against injustices can all be curtailed if the larger group—the state—chooses. Individual right to life as such does not exist; abortion, murder of political dissidents, suppression of religious practice take place as the state thinks them necessary. All of these practices flow from the basic view that the human person exists for the good of the group.

One final example from our exercise is that of the atheistic existentialist. This philosophy is very individualistic and pragmatic. Jean-Paul Sartre wrote that a certain amount of the absurdity of life can be overcome when the individual chooses to be himself or herself, but as the choice is made a feeling of aloneness and despair still results. No one can help us, not even God. Some existentialists who accept this view of reality (though this was not the case for Sartre himself) see no reason to help better the condition of humanity. What is the sense of working for peace or justice, what meaning is there to cleaning up a polluted environment, why be concerned about the starving poor? Since we as individuals are fundamentally and radically alone, why bother with social concerns?

A PLURALISTIC SOCIETY

These various philosophies, and many others as well, compete for the attention of today's Christian. We live in a pluralistic society. There are many viewpoints about what it means to be human and just as many views of what is right and what is wrong. Exactly who is worth paying attention to and whom should we ignore?

WHO IS RIGHT?

The following statements have been made by various people in our society:

1. When a person becomes a burden on society, for example, the senile and the hopelessly retarded, society should have the right to terminate that person's life.
2. Why go to church? Religion is no more than a superstitious carry-over from the past.
3. The most worthwhile goal in life is to amass as much money as possible. Nothing else really matters.
4. Why should we have to pay taxes for so many social programs? Most poor people are just lazy and merely freeload off those of us who work.
5. A couple should live together before they are married. How else will they know if they are compatible?
6. Why not cheat on income taxes? Everyone else does.
7. What I do with my time and my money is nobody else's business.
8. If people aren't happy living together as husband and wife, they should be allowed to get a "no fault" divorce. No questions asked.

Discuss:

1. Identify the kind of person in our society who might say each of the above. Have you ever heard these opinions expressed? How often? By whom?

2. The Catholic church teaches that all of these statements are wrong for one reason or another. For each statement, give at least one reason why it might be wrong.

One idea clearly emerges: If we do not formulate our own philosophy, we may fall into accepting one which is not Christian. We should not easily and unthinkingly accept everything that comes along. Christians have a definite vision of what the human person is and should act according to that vision. We should be very reluctant to accept what others in our society might like us to be—whether it is a pleasure machine, a cog in a smooth-functioning operation or an isolated individual.

GOOD IN SOCIETY

However, we should also be aware of the many good voices in the world, voices that will help us live a life in accordance with the Christian view of the human person.

Certainly Christian teaching doesn't hold that everyone is wrong except those who follow our way of doing things. The Christian community doesn't require us to quit thinking or to surrender our personal freedom. There is much good in the world, even though it is in no way associated with the visible church. Medical research centers, CARE, the Red Cross and countless other agencies and programs bring much good to people. Being a Catholic in our pluralistic society does not mean that we should shut our eyes to the good in the world. On the contrary, we should be willing and ready to actively join hands with people everywhere who are striving for the betterment of humanity.

My dear people,
let us love one another
since love comes from God
and everyone who loves is begotten by God and
knows God.
Anyone who fails to love can never have known God,
because God is love (1 Jn 4:7-8).

The Second Vatican Council also reminds us of the goodness and worth of all people everywhere. We are called not only to recognize the goodness in the world, but to work actively in and with all those elements in society which foster human dignity and which work toward overcoming such things as disease and poverty. The Vatican II document, *Pastoral Constitution on the Modern World,* states it this way:

> When circumstances of time and place create the need, she [the Church] can and indeed should initiate activities on behalf of all men. This is particularly true of activities designed for the needy, such as the works of mercy and similar undertakings. . . . The Church further recognizes that worthy elements are found in today's social movements. . . . The Council, therefore looks with great respect upon all the true, good, and just elements found in the very wide variety of institutions which the human race has established for itself and constantly continues to establish. The Council affirms, moreover, that the Church is willing to assist and promote all these institutions to the extent that such a service depends on her and can be associated with her mission. She has no fiercer desire than that, in pursuit of the welfare of all, she may be able to develop herself freely under any kind of government which grants recognition to the basic rights of person and family and to the demands of the common good (No. 42).

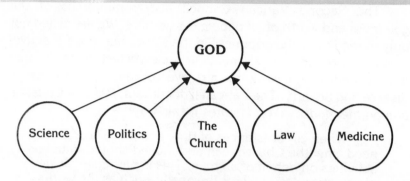

Christians see that all those who are working for the betterment of human life are working for God's cause. Christians are unique among all these groups, however, because we believe and proclaim that Jesus Christ is the fullness of all that humanity is striving for, and that the world will eventually overcome all suffering in him alone.

Discuss ways in which the church has actively worked in your community to help others. What are some things that the church has *not* done which need to be done in your community?

List ways each of the activities diagrammed above help work for God's kingdom.

The different groups in a pluralistic society, each trying to be true to its own convictions, form a living society. We Christians must take a vital and active place in the larger community by being faithful to Jesus Christ. This mission cannot be accomplished if we yield to every force in society, if we become invisible by becoming no different from those who are not Christian.

Christians are fundamentally realistic. We believe that there is good in the world, but we also recognize that there is sin in the world and that the world is in need of redemption. The world needs Jesus Christ, his message and the values which flow from his message. The world needs to hear the truth from the Christian community—salvation is found only in Jesus Christ.

Our pluralistic society, then, speaks with many voices; some call us to good while others call us to evil. The Christian is one who decides his or her own course in life, knowing full well that not to decide is to decide. The Christian accepts the vision of God which sees others as neighbor and self as endowed with tremendous dignity. We will look more closely at the Christian view of who we are in the next chapter.

SUMMARY

1. There are many different philosophies of the human person. They include:

    a. an Oriental view which emphasizes submissiveness to the cosmic scheme

    b. a hedonistic view of pleasure seeking

    c. a communistic view of submission to the group

    d. an existentialistic view of absolute freedom and isolation

    e. a nihilistic view which denies that life has any meaning

    f. a humanistic view which ignores the spiritual dimension

    g. a Christian view of loving service to others

2. Our concept of who we are is important for us to determine because it affects the way we act toward others—whether we know it or not.

3. Modern media try to sell particular philosophies. These views often make the human person an object who is to be judged merely by external appearances.

4. Each philosophy competing for our attention suggests certain ways we should act and certain attitudes we should have. We will unconsciously pick up these attitudes and suggested actions unless we evaluate critically the philosophies which bombard us.

5. There is much good in the world. We should all work together to further those causes which foster human dignity.

6. The Christian takes the time and effort to measure a particular view of the human person against the Christian concept of the human person.

ACTIVITIES

1. Bring to class ads clipped from magazines or newspapers. You might also select a contemporary record or two. In addition, consider taping commercials from television or the radio for this exercise.

   a. Observe what each ad is trying to sell on the surface level; for example, soda pop commercials sell soft drinks; automobile ads sell particular cars.

   b. Re-examine the ads to note the assumptions they make about the human person. For example, some soft drink commercials are really promoting the concept of "youthful vigor"; some liquor commercials are selling "prestige and success"; some car ads are making blatant pitches to sexual prowess.

2. The following exercise is designed for you to examine your values and to try to understand where you get them.

   a. Write a short essay responding to the question, What do I consider a successful life for me?

   b. If you want, share your essay with several other members of your class.

   c. Discuss or think about these questions:

      • What is *success*?

      • Look at your view of a successful life. What has influenced you?

      • Are these good or bad influences?

   Note that your view of your future says something about how you view what is good for people in general.

3. Consider this definition of Christian morality by Sertillanges (quoted by Father Marc Oraison in *Morality for Our Times*): Morality is "the science of what man ought to be by reason of what he is."

  a. If morality is a science, then like any other science it is by definition open-ended. Does that mean that our application of moral principles to new situations can change? For example, can Christians today tolerate slavery or the subjugation of women in light of our current understanding of equality?

  b. If morality is based on the search for norms of free human conduct in light of what we are, how important is it for us to have a good definition of ourselves? Will a Christian view the human person differently from a Hindu or an atheist? Why? Where does a Christian get a good definition of who we are?

VALUES AND A PHILOSOPHY OF LIFE

Introduction: Your values often give a clue to how you view yourself and others. If your values are in conflict, perhaps you are not sure which philosophy of life you want to live by. If your values are superficial, perhaps your view of yourself, others and life in general needs some change.

Try the following classic exercise in values clarification: Take no more than 10 minutes to list the 10 things you prize or cherish more than anything else in the world. You don't have to share your list with anyone if you don't want to.

1._____   6._____

2._____   7._____

3._____   8._____

4._____   9._____

5._____   10. _____

When you finish your list, code your responses according to the following:

★ items that are possessions

P items that are persons

$ items which cost a lot of money—you decide what "a lot of money" means

R items that reflect religious values (love, justice, peace, etc.)

F items which you think your friends share in common with you

Reflection: Write a short essay which explains what your values reveal about your philosophy of life.

TWO

Who Are You?— A Christian Response

Everyone moved by the Spirit is a son of God. The spirit you received is not the spirit of slaves bringing fear into your lives again; it is the spirit of sons, and it makes us cry out, "Abba, Father!" The Spirit himself and our spirit bear united witness that we are children of God. And if we are children we are heirs as well: heirs of God and coheirs with Christ, sharing his sufferings so as to share his glory.

—St. Paul

In the last chapter we saw how some people view the human person. In this chapter we will analyze another way to answer the question of human identity—a Christian response. The Christian vision of who we are is unique. When this vision is accepted, it helps us to relate to others in such a way that we are truly responding to the call of God.

There are three basic ways by which the Christian is given some help in defining the human person. The first is from the way things are, that is, *from the nature of things.* How we are made as persons reveals something about us. This has been called many things, most often natural law or natural revelation.

A second help in arriving at our self-definition comes *from what God has revealed to us through the history of the Jewish people.* This history is recorded in the Old Testament. It tells the partial story of salvation history, God's way of working in history. Our faith in God's word as revealed in salvation history tells us something about ourselves that we cannot necessarily reason to.

25

A third source of the Christian concept of the human per-son comes to us *from the word spoken to us by God the Father through his Son, Jesus Christ*. The Father wishes to tell us about himself, ourselves and our relationships with others. Thus, he sent his Son to speak to us through his words and actions. In a special way, too, Jesus communicated some powerful truths through his suffering, death, resurrection and glorification.

In this chapter we shall analyze each one of these sources of a Christian concept of who we are.

NATURAL LAW

Teilhard de Chardin, a great 20th-century Catholic thinker, said that because we are the only creatures in God's creation who "know that we know," we are able to discover many things about ourselves through *reason*. We are able to discover the divine plan for things, including ourselves, by looking at how we are made; the way we are is a clue to what we should be. Thus, natural law offers some answers to the question of who we are: We are rational, free, loving, embodied, unique yet social, and historical creatures.

Rational

One of the first truths we discover about ourselves is that we can think. Though this seems obvious, it is rationality which enables us to figure out problems, discover laws within nature, reflect on the meaning of things and the like. It is this ability more than any other which has helped humans progress. We have benefited from the collective wisdom and learning of the men and women who came before us.

Free

Another fundamental human trait is the ability to choose. Unlike animals who are bound by instinct, we have a certain amount of freedom to change, to improve our lot, to direct our futures. In more traditional terms this ability is known as *free will*. It enables us to choose between good and evil.

Though psychology has shown that a great deal of our

behavior is determined by our heredity and environment, almost all social scientists admit that we do have a certain freedom of choice. True, we cannot control the environment we were born into; nor do we have much control over the kind of body we have, with its various hereditary strengths and weaknesses. But we still have a certain degree of freedom to affect (change) the world around us and to work with the particular talents we've been given.

For example, you may have been born into a family and a society which is extremely bigoted toward members of another race. Perhaps you were taught to be prejudiced and discriminatory to members of this race. But you still have the freedom to discover for yourself about "those" people. You have the ability to think for yourself, read, talk to others, and then use your freedom to become more tolerant and loving of all peoples.

REFLECTION

Our capacity to reason and to choose separates us from other creatures. Traditionally these two faculties are at the heart of human nature; they comprise our soul. They are spiritual qualities which are difficult to measure, difficult to analyze. And yet they are real and help define who we are. What would you say to a person who holds the following? Would you agree or disagree? Why? Discuss.

- Because a fetus can't think, it is not really human.
- Retarded people are only half human because they have very low IQs.
- A comatose patient is only a vegetable.
- Hopeless drug addicts, slaves to their habits, have surrendered their humanity.

Discuss:

1. Are we human when we sleep? If you answer yes, can you use the same argument to defend the humanity of unborn infants, retarded people and comatose patients? Explain.
2. If a human brain could be kept alive in a glass container, would it still be a human being? Explain and defend your answer.

Loving

One of the proofs that we are indeed free is that we can choose to do good to another person. If we desire the good of another person, we love. It takes freedom to love. Experience tells us that we are capable of loving or not loving.

In one sense, love is the highest form of choosing; this is so because it is choosing "for" other people. Choosing for others means advancing their well-being, making sure they grow, creating the atmosphere in which good things happen. In choosing for others, we may well have to sacrifice our own comfort and convenience. This ability is unique to us humans.

Perhaps a story will best illustrate this point. One day, so the story goes, a visitor went with Mother Teresa of Calcutta as she searched the streets for people abandoned and dying. They came upon a person covered with open sores and lying in the filth of the gutter. Mother Teresa immediately lifted the dying person and began to care for him. The visitor drew back and said, "I wouldn't touch that person for a million dollars." Mother Teresa answered, "Neither would I." Love, choosing for others, is a powerful gift.

Embodied

We are people with bodies. This seems obvious, but it is an important truth for truly understanding the human person. Some thinkers throughout history have maintained that our true identity is spiritual; for them, the body is a necessary evil which we must endure and even try to escape.

But we are not human beings without our bodies. We will see in the next chapter that our having a body manifests our relationship to the rest of created reality. We can only become ourselves through the bodies we have. We know things through our five senses. We express ourselves and experience reality through our emotions, our desires and drives, our feelings and our likes and dislikes. All of these help make us who we are; all have implications for our choices.

Unique, Yet Social

Each of us is unique. We are unlike any other person, past, present or future. And yet, despite the fact of our uniqueness, we are social beings. Our uniqueness shines forth only in community with others. What a great paradox that is! We can only become ourselves when we relate to others as individuals in the great human family.

Historical

As human beings we each have a history. We sum up in our humanity all who have preceded us. The first question a person with amnesia asks is "Who am I?" Amnesiacs do not know themselves because they do not know their past. We are our past.

In the same way, the human race has a memory. To be an American—or German, Australian, Nicaraguan or whatever nationality—is to live in openness to those who have gone before us; their history is our history. We are part of the flow which is humanity. We add to the progress of the race by handing on our talents, insights and values to the future. We are within the community of humankind and potentially can add significantly to it.

FAMILY TREE

(childhood events)

great-grandparents	xx	xx	xx	xx		great waves of immigration; era of rapid industrialization
grandparents	x	x	x	x		World War I; cars and radios become widely available
parents		x		x		World War II and Korean Conflict; jet travel changes modes of transportation; television changes our systems of communications and entertainment; "Space Age" begins
YOU			x			computers and high technology change our lifestyle and our society

(your children)

(your grand-
children)

Reflection. Each of us is a genetic blend of all those who have preceded us. We carry on the flow of humanity. In the three generations before you, 14 people were involved in bringing you into existence; in four generations, 30 people; in five generations—100 years more or less—62 people! This simple illustration underscores our continuity with humanity. We are links in a chain. We have been formed by our individual and collective pasts and we shall in turn form the future. But this is not the whole story. As we shall see, if we use our freedom properly, we pass on more than our own makeup to a genetic pool; we pass on the fruits of our wisdom and love as well.

You and Your Family. It might be interesting for you to investigate your family tree. Interview relatives and try to discover your cultural heritage. Are you proud of it? What good traits have you inherited from your family? Share these with your classmates.

To sum up this section, then, we can see that natural law tells us quite a bit about ourselves. Our human reason can discover that we are thinking beings with bodies; we are unique individuals, but individuals who are related to others in community. We are historical beings endowed with free will which enables us to choose and to choose "for" others—to love.

FOR ANALYSIS

Discuss the following situations. Remember, something is wrong if it violates our human nature.

1. A high school coach has a very good team. It is up against some stiff competition, however. During a break he gives the players oranges with some "power boosters" (drugs) added. "It's just a help to them," he explains, "a way of bringing the team to its best possible performance level."

2. Mr. Johnson makes $50,000 a year and pays $14,000 in taxes. He has four kids. His wife is not employed. Would it be wrong for him to give half his remaining salary to the poor? (When you discuss this, think of the consequences for his family of living on $18,000 a year.)

OLD TESTAMENT REVELATION

The word of God written into the nature of things is not the only way by which we discover our identity. The word of God found in the Old Testament also reveals to us certain things about our identity. Through Old Testament revelation we learn that we are the image of God, fundamentally good, and God's partners.

Image of God

A most striking revelation about our true identity comes from the book of Genesis.

God created man in the image of himself,
in the image of God he created him,
male and female he created them (Gn 1:27).

What a tremendous truth this is! By being created in the image of God, our very activities of thinking and loving, in fact our very being, reflect the beauty, the wisdom, the love of the Creator. What incredible value we must have in God's sight! We reflect his glory and each of us is of tremendous worth to him.

Fundamentally Good

Reading further along in Genesis we note that "God saw all he had made, and indeed it was very good" (Gn 1:31). It is precisely because we are the image of God that we are fundamentally good. What a refreshing thought this is in comparison to those philosophies of life that hold that we are evil and have little worth or dignity. Because we know that we are good at the very core of our being, we should be a hopeful people, especially in regard to our final destiny.

There is one important implication which flows from an understanding of humanity as an image of God which reflects his goodness: The more we act according to the way we are made, the more we reflect the image of God our Creator. A quotation from St. Irenaeus underscores this point: "The glory of God is man fully alive." We give glory to God by being fully human, that is, by being what our Lord God made us to be. We are not, as taught in a more pessimistic philosophy of life, mere clods of earth. We are reflections, images of the Creator.

We should mention here, though, that part of our Christian view of the person is that we are fallen creatures who have sinned and are capable of doing evil. There is no denying that we are diamonds in the rough; we as individuals and as a human family need lots of work to allow God's image to shine through. Any philosophy which denies human weakness and the reality of evil is unrealistic. God's creatures, made in his image and reflecting his very dignity, are capable of doing evil, are capable of distorting their true identity.

EXERCISE

Look at today's newspaper. Find five stories which show that people are basically good. Find five which show that people are basically evil. Bring them to class. Which were easier to find? Is it easy to believe in our basic goodness? Why or why not? Is it easier to believe in the basic goodness of the people you meet every day? Why or why not?

God's Partners

In that same first chapter of Genesis we discover that we are God's partners. "God blessed them, saying to them 'Be fruitful, multiply, fill the earth and conquer it'" (Gn 1:28). We are in a very real sense co-creators with God because we have been given dominion which we must rule, develop and take care of. In the practical order, what this means is that we must share in the development of the world.

"The fish of the sea, the birds of the air, and all living things that move on the earth" have been given for our use and betterment. We are caretakers who are to use the rest of creation to develop ourselves and, in doing so, to draw closer to our Creator. Using creation, of course, does not mean abusing it. We are not, for example, meant to rape the environment. We are to cooperate in the divine plan by developing, expanding and properly using the goods of the earth which have been given to us.

STEWARDSHIP

Stewards are those who take care of something entrusted to them. Being co-creators with God our Father means being good stewards. Mark the following poll which deals with questions of stewardship. Discuss the questions which follow.

	Agree	Dis-agree	?
1. The government should spend as much money as necessary to set up space colonies.	☐	☐	☐
2. During an energy crisis the government should allow strip mining of coal.	☐	☐	☐
3. No expense should be spared in trying to find a cure for cancer.	☐	☐	☐
4. Efforts to save endangered species of animals should be stepped up.	☐	☐	☐
5. We should support nuclear energy to meet the needs of the 21st century.	☐	☐	☐
6. New medical techniques should be used even if some people die in the experimental stages.	☐	☐	☐

Discuss:

1. Give some arguments for and against each of the positions above.
2. Can you think of some examples of tampering with the laws of nature which would be clearly immoral?

NEW TESTAMENT REVELATION

Our most basic belief as Christians is that Jesus of Nazareth is the Son of God. In Jesus, God the Father poured himself out and became united with his creation through the great and profound mystery of the incarnation. God became one of us in the person of his Son, Jesus Christ. We cannot begin to grasp the depth of the mystery which is the incarnation, but we can note a few startling implications.

First, when God became one of us in order to share, indeed to give his very life for us, he showed what tremendous worth we have in his eyes. Because Jesus Christ died, we have been given superabundant life. We live because the Father loves us so much he gave his Son to us.

Second, in giving himself to us there is a great mystery of love. God became one of us, he actually entered our history and is part of our world. He is literally *Emmanuel,* "God with us."

Third, we have a special relationship with God revealed when the apostles asked Jesus how they should pray. Jesus taught them the Our Father. He told the disciples, and he tells us, that we can dare to address God by the same intimate word which he himself used: *Abba,* "daddy." We have become adopted sons and daughters of God, and we are in union with our brother, Lord and Savior, Jesus Christ.

This relationship is earthshaking. If indeed we are sons and daughters of the Father by adoption and Jesus is our brother—and our faith tells us this is so—then we are brothers and sisters to one another. We are not isolated individuals in a common herd which is humanity; we are members of one family with God as our Father. And if this is what we are, and there is no reason to doubt the word of Jesus, then we can easily understand how we ought to relate to one another. We must treat one another as brothers and sisters.

The gift of the Holy Spirit given to us at baptism helps us to accept the truth of our common brotherhood and sisterhood. This Spirit, the gift of love of the Father and Son to us, binds us together into this family, into the body of Jesus Christ. This same Spirit of truth enables us to live our true identity in joy, peace, patience, charity, gladness and friendliness.

When Jesus taught his disciples about the Last Judgment, he most certainly had in mind the kind of unity which we should have as members of one family:

> "When the Son of Man comes in his glory, escorted by all the angels, then he will take his seat on his throne of glory. All the nations will be assembled before him and he will separate men one from another as the

shepherd separates sheep from goats. He will place the sheep on his right hand and the goats on his left. Then the King will say to those on his right hand, 'Come, you whom my Father has blessed, take for your heritage the kingdom prepared for you since the foundation of the world. For I was hungry and you gave me drink; I was a stranger and you made me welcome; naked and you clothed me, sick and you visited me, in prison and you came to see me.' Then the virtuous will say to him in reply, 'Lord, when did we see you a stranger and make you welcome; naked and clothe you; sick or in prison and go to see you?' And the King will answer, 'I tell you solemnly, in so far as you did this to one of the least of these brothers of mine, you did it to me' " (Mt 25:31-40).

SUMMARY

If it is true that our concept of the human person helps us to determine how we ought to act toward others, what are some concrete implications for those of us who accept the Christian view as set forth in this chapter?

But first, let us summarize. People can use their minds to discover that humans

- have the ability to think and to choose. The first trait enables us to pass on wisdom and figure out problems; the second enables us to choose our own destiny and to love.

- are embodied creatures who are in continuity with other people who came before and after us; we are historical beings.

- are unique, each endowed with certain gifts and abilities, but at the same time dependent on others, social by nature.

Furthermore, we Christians believe that God revealed that we are

- his very image and, as such, fundamentally good, though prone to sin.

- his partners, co-creators with him.

- adopted members of his family, brothers and sisters to Jesus and to one another.

Here, then, are three implications which flow from this concept of the human person:

1. When we think and when we choose, especially when we choose to love, we become who we are meant to be. The more fully human we become, the more we reflect the God who created us. To lessen our ability to think or our ability to choose and to love dehumanizes us; it is wrong, immoral. For example, we are acting as an image of God when we study or work for a living. Why? Simply because studying and working can be very moral actions that help develop human potential. In studying we reflect God's image; by working we co-create with him. On the other hand, it is immoral to foolishly surrender our ability to think by taking harmful drugs for kicks or by drinking to excess. By doing so we give up part of what it means to be a human being made in God's image.

2. Because we are social beings, we have tremendous responsibilities in regard to others. We should "subdue the earth" for the benefit of all and in so doing allow God's creative nature to shine forth for all peoples. We are not islands; on the contrary, we live in relationship to other people and the rest of our environment. We must do our best to live in harmony. For example, it is wrong to pollute the atmosphere or hoard food while others starve. These actions disregard our partnership with our God and abuse, rather than use, the beautiful creation he gave to us.

3. Finally, our destiny and movement toward God must include loving and relating to all persons, even to the "least of these." Morality is not an individual affair between each of us and God. We are members of a family united in Christ our Lord. To be Christian is to relate to our brothers and sisters everywhere, to treat others the way we would like to be treated.

ACTIVITIES

A. *Case for Discussion:*

The mayor of a medium-sized city in the United States says that an armed populace is a deterrent to crime. He says that "every home should have a weapon to protect the individuals who reside there." He claims that arming is a constitutional right and has urged his city commission to adopt a resolution to declare a war on crime.

The police chief is against the idea. The chief maintains that "when you ask a community to arm itself, you're asking for trouble."

Questions:

1. Where do you stand on this issue?

2. List arguments for and against the mayor's position:

   For

   a. _____

   b. _____

   c. _____

   Against

   a. _____

   b. _____

   c. _____

3. Based on a Christian concept of the human person, would the mayor's proposal be right or wrong? Explain your answer.

B. *Self-Reflection:* Reflect on your self-image and see how it matches the Christian concept of the human person. Answer these questions about yourself.

1. You are God's image. Name two gifts which you have been given that can help others see the goodness of God in the world.

2. You are fundamentally good.

   a. What is the best thing about you?

   b. What fault do you need to work on which keeps your goodness from shining forth to others?

3. What does it mean for you personally to be able to call God *Abba*?

THREE

Relationship and Responsibility

Liberty means responsibility. That is why most men dread it.
—George Bernard Shaw

Jesus constantly rebuked the Pharisees for their legalism, their tendency to overemphasize external observance of the law. At times they forgot that the essence of morality is doing God's will. Legalism is an ever-present danger. Each of us must constantly try to keep first things first in the realm of morality. This involves a concept of morality which keeps the spirit as well as the letter of the law.

One way we can avoid a legalistic attitude is by remembering that all morality is rooted in love. This chapter examines morality as *a free (and hence responsible) response to the love relationship we have with all others as our brothers and sisters in Christ.* Let's begin our discussion by considering the following incident and what it reveals to us about the kind of responsibility that always accompanies friendship.

A CASE FOR DISCUSSION

Your best friend has been accused of cheating on an important exam. As a result, she is informed, she will fail the course. *You* are the one who cheated, but you say nothing and let your friend take the blame and the severe penalty which you deserve.

1. Which is more wrong—cheating on the test or allowing a friend to be hurt?

2. If you said that the more serious offense is hurting your friend, what is the reason for your answer? Is there a law that says you cannot hurt your friends? Is there something in friendship itself that tells you what you did was wrong?

3. Is a failure in friendship a kind of failure in love? Does all love imply some kind of relationship for which we are responsible?

4. Do you think that what we do to others not only affects our relationship with them but also our relationship with God? In other words, can we hurt our relationship with others without at the same time hurting our relationship with God?

THE MORAL DIMENSION OF RELATIONSHIPS

In the last chapter we saw that our ability to reason about ourselves helps us discover that human beings are rational, free and loving. A key implication flows from this discovery: The *human* dimension of our relationships with others is determined by our capacity to *know* what is loving or unloving and then freely to *choose* between the two. Thus, when we knowingly and freely relate to another in a loving way, we are acting morally; when we freely and knowingly relate to another in an unloving way, we act immorally. In the example given above, if we knowingly and freely allow our friend to suffer a punishment which we deserve, we commit an unloving and consequently immoral act.

LOVE

Discuss why each kind of love listed below is important to full human growth and development. Give specific examples of the destructive effects associated with the abuse or neglect of each of these kinds of love.

- love of pleasure (food, comfort, etc.)
- a parent's love for a child
- a child's love for his or her parents
- love for school or country
- emotional, sexual love
- love for oneself
- friendship
- love of God

RELATIONSHIPS IN THE WORLD OF NATURE

Animals relate to one another in a wide variety of ways. But relationships among animals are quite different from human relationships. By looking at how animal and human relationships differ we can better understand what is distinctively moral about our relationships to one another as human beings.

Because we are endowed with intellects and free wills we can know right from wrong, and we have the power to choose between the two. Animals, however, possess neither intellect nor free will. This is not to say that animals do not act in extraordinary ways: A hive of bees, a highly trained dog or a killer whale may amaze us with what it is able to do. But there is no evidence to indicate that animals consciously know what they are doing or reflect on their actions in the same way humans do. Nor is there reason to believe that animals can recognize two ways of acting, one wrong and the other right, and make free choices between them. None of us, for example, would claim that animals should be held morally responsible for what they do. A lion, for example, is not responsible for killing its prey, nor is the butterfly responsible for taking nectar from a flower.

Similarly, animals lack the capacity to establish love relationships. The mating rituals of some animals as well as the way they care for and defend their young exhibit what might look like love, but this "love" is instinctive rather than the free, knowing love that we humans experience and for which we are responsible. A mother cat, for example, is no more responsible for the care she gives her kittens than she is for killing a mouse. It is purely a matter of a cat being a cat.

In short, we human beings are unique among all the creatures of the earth. Although we too possess instinctive drives—hunger, sex, self-defense, and the like—we also possess an intellect and free will. These enable us to direct our drives. We can reflect on our actions and choose ways that are loving; we can avoid unloving acts and attitudes which destroy the happiness and well-being of others.

DISCUSS

1. "Where there is no freedom, there is no responsibility. Where there is no responsibility, there is no morality." Do you agree? Why or why not?

2. In court cases involving murder, a plea of temporary insanity is often entered for the defendant in the hope of avoiding the death penalty or a life sentence. How does this relate to what was said above regarding intellect, free will and responsibility?

3. Compare your relationship to your brothers and sisters with the relationship of kittens in a litter. What does it mean to say that you do not choose your brothers and sisters, but you do choose whether or not you will relate to them in a loving way?

4. Rank the following according to degree of responsibility. The number 1 represents the greatest degree of responsibility.

   _____The person who drops a bomb.

   _____The person who designed the plane.

   _____The officer who ordered the air strike.

_____The person who paid taxes.

_____The person who maintains the plane.

_____The person who built the bomb.

REVELATION AND MORAL RESPONSIBILITY

Until now our reflections have been restricted to what the natural law reveals about relationships and responsibility. Well-intentioned but non-believing humanists could accept what we have concluded about intellect, free will and moral responsibility. But we Christians believe that a Christian view of the human person and moral responsibility is perfected by a knowledge of God's revelation of who we are in relationship to him, to ourselves, and to one another.

The Old Testament

A fundamental and significant divine revelation appears in the opening chapter of the Bible where it is written that after creating all the things of nature,

> God created man in the image of himself
> in the image of God he created him (Gn 1:27).

According to Christian revelation we are unique among all of God's creatures; we alone are created in a relationship of likeness to God. Because we are like God, we are free. And, because we are free, we are responsible for the relationship we have with God. The Genesis story of Adam and Eve before the fall reveals the kind of relationship God wills for us. Adam and Eve were on intimate and harmonious terms with God; the Lord cared for them and came to visit them much as a father would come to visit his children. This harmony with God enabled Adam and Eve to live peacefully with each other and with the world around them.

The theme of responsibility for the relationship we have with God is symbolically represented in God's command to Adam and Eve not to eat from the tree that stood in the middle of the garden which God had created for them. When they disobeyed God they failed to be responsible for the love relationship they had with him. In doing this they experienced loss and confusion; they no longer possessed the happiness and freedom which God willed them to have in relationship to him. This loss of intimacy with God is dramatically emphasized when the scriptures tell us that Adam and Eve were ashamed and tried to hide from God.

After firmly establishing morality within the context of our relationship to God, Genesis goes on to reveal a second great truth: Our responsibility to God cannot be separated from our responsibility to one another. Thus, after the fall, Adam and Eve were not only ashamed in God's presence, but were also ashamed to be naked in the presence of each other.

An even more dramatic instance of the breakdown in human relationships which results from the breakdown of the relationship with God is recounted in the story of Cain and Abel:

> Cain said to his brother Abel, "Let us go out"; and while they were in the open country, Cain set on his brother Abel and killed him.
> Yahweh asked Cain, "Where is your brother Abel?" "I do not know" he replied. "Am I my brother's guardian?" (Gn 4:8-9).

In Exodus God offers an emphatic response to Cain's famous question. Yes, we are the keepers of our brothers and sisters. We are responsible for our relationship with others. To have a relationship with God means that we must nurture our relationships with others. Responsibility to God involves responsibility to others. Exodus expresses this theme beautifully when it tells the story of Yahweh establishing a *covenant* with his people on Mt. Sinai.

God's covenant, his loving contract with his people, reveals that he is and always will be faithful to us. He never wavers in his love for us. He will never fail to be responsible for the children he creates in his image and likeness. In response to his love for us, God asks that we renew our fidelity to him by obeying his loving will. He desires that his children love him. The first three commandments suggest the ways we should respond to God's unconditional love: We should give him priority in our lives; we should respect his name; we should worship him.

The seven remaining commandments instruct us to demonstrate our fidelity to God by loving others. God wills that we refrain from all hurtful and unjust acts, and even unloving desires. Just as weakening our relationship with God brings about a weakening in our relationship with others, so too our failures to love others result in a weakening in our relationship to God. We are first responsible to God. Whenever we sin, we sin against him. This is most clearly seen in the first three commandments. But the last seven commandments drive home the important truth that in loving his children we truly express our love for God.

REFLECTION

Read Genesis 2:4-25 carefully and list the ways God showed his love to Adam and Eve. Then read Genesis 3 and note the specific effects that eating the forbidden fruit had on Adam and Eve's relationship with God, with one another, and with the world around them.

The New Testament

In the New Testament, Jesus unites the love of God to the love of neighbor. When asked which of the commandments was the greatest, Jesus responded:

"This is the first: *Listen, Israel, the Lord our God is the one Lord, and you must love the Lord your God with all your heart, with all your soul,* with all your mind and *with all your strength.* The second is this: *You must love your neighbor as yourself.* There is no commandment greater than these" (Mk 12:29-31).

Jesus, of course, is God united with humanity; he is God-made-man. As the second person of the Trinity, Jesus is God-in-our-midst, the Word made flesh. The historical Jesus demonstrated that he was aware of and responsive to his unique relationship with God. In everything he did he always sought to do the Father's will. And he shared this relationship with his Father by loving everyone he met with the Father's unconditional love.

In the words of our Lord at the Last Supper we are told of the intimate relationship he wills to have with us:

"As the Father has loved me,
so I have loved you.
remain in my love.
If you keep my commandments
you will remain in my love,
just as I have kept my Father's commandments
and remain in his love.
I have told you this
so that my own joy may be in you
and your joy be complete" (Jn 15:9-11).

Jesus then directs us to the secret of his joy:

"This is my commandment:
love one another
as I have loved you" (Jn 15:12).

Here we approach the foundation of all Christian morality: *By loving everyone with Christlike love, we experience a bond with everyone we love; more important, we experience an intimate union with the Lord himself.*

MORE REFLECTION

Read and discuss the following texts. How do they demonstrate that the love of God is to be united to the love of neighbor?

Matthew 5:23-24   Matthew 18:23-25

1 John 4:7-12   Romans 12:9-21

JESUS GIVES US THE SPIRIT

We have seen that Jesus calls us to a new responsibility of loving others as he loves us. The relationship of love that unites us to God and others is not merely a moral idea. Rather, it is the result of the Holy Spirit who has been sent by the Lord to dwell in us and thus make us one with him.

The Holy Spirit is the spirit of love who binds together the Father and the Son within the Trinity. To be given the Holy Spirit is to be given the love which unites the Father and Son into a community. Thus, to possess the Spirit is to be related to God in a unique bond of love which we in turn should extend to others by loving them as Jesus loves us.

The Holy Spirit comes to us at baptism. The gift of the Spirit remains with us like a seed that needs to grow through a lifetime of faith in Christ and daily love for others. In a deep and mysterious sense the person of the Holy Spirit is the foundation of Christian morality. In the Spirit we share in the Lord's relationship with his Father. Through the action of the Spirit in our lives we can extend God's love to others.

When St. Paul writes about the central importance of love—the greatest gift of the Holy Spirit—he gives us one of the most beautiful and frequently quoted passages of scripture. This passage describes in a sublime way the *Christian* meaning of love:

Love is always patient and kind; it is never jealous; love is never boastful or conceited; it is never rude or selfish; it does not take offense, and is not resentful. Love takes no pleasure in other people's sins but delights in the truth; it is always ready to excuse, to trust, to hope, and to endure whatever comes (1 Cor 13:4-7).

None of us perfectly measures up to this kind of love. But the Spirit of Love given to us by Jesus draws us toward an ever greater degree of this Christlike love. The Spirit helps us see others as our brothers and sisters. It impels us to seek the good of others as much as we do our own. It even makes it possible for us to love our enemies.

SOME APPLICATIONS

A. *Read Acts 2:1-24.* This account of Pentecost shows the powerful effect the Holy Spirit had on the early Christians. Discuss as a class the change the Spirit brought about in the disciples. Also read about St. Paul's conversion, Acts 9:1-27, and compare the changes brought about in Paul to the experience of the apostles at Pentecost.

B. *Imagine the following scene:*

> You are walking with a friend when suddenly you come upon a group of men assaulting a person around your own age. Both you and your friend begin shouting for help, but you don't interfere because you are afraid you might get hurt yourselves. Then you realize that the person being beaten is your own younger brother. Instantly you forget what could happen to you, and you rush to the thugs and try to stop them.

1. How did the sudden recognition of your relationship to the victim affect your responsibility to him?

2. Jesus teaches that we are all brothers and sisters. Does this apply even to the thugs who have attacked your brother? Are they also your brothers in Christ? What is your responsibility to them?

SUMMARY

1. Natural law tells us that humans are capable of moral acts because we are rational, free and able to love.

2. Because animals cannot reason and are bound by instinct, the concept of morality does not apply to them.

3. The Old Testament reveals that our relationship to one another cannot be separated from our relationship with God.

4. Christian morality is rooted in our relationship to Jesus Christ who commanded us to love others as he loved us.

5. The gift of the Holy Spirit opens us to the experience of the risen Lord and helps us express our relationship with Christ in our daily relationships with others.

6. Here are two definitions of morality which have been covered in these first three chapters:

• Morality is the science of what we ought to be by reason of who we are.

• Morality is a free response to the love relationship we have with all others as our brothers and sisters in Jesus Christ.

ACTIVITIES

A. Read a short biography of one of the saints and report on how his or her relationship with Christ was acted out in the way he or she cared for others.

B. Interview your parents and ask them how their faith has helped them in their relationship with each other, with you, and with your brothers and sisters. Compare and contrast responses with your classmates.

C. A Case for Discussion:

Some people have observed that there seems to be a growing disrespect for the law not only in this country but worldwide. In our major cities drivers run stop signs and red lights. On the highways the speed limit is often exceeded. People cheat on their income taxes and fail to report "under the table" payments for services rendered. The criminal justice system seems to do little to punish the users of certain illegal drugs like marijuana and cocaine.

In light of these and similar flagrant disregard of the law, some people claim that more and more people lack respect for the very reason for law: to protect people who live together in community, who live in relationship.

Irresponsibility seems to be an evergrowing phenomenon.

The solution proposed by these critics? Much stiffer punishment for abusers of the law. One columnist argues that very stiff penalties should be inflicted on pot users, for example, lengthy imprisonment. If people won't freely accept responsibility for their actions, then they should be forced to do so, these critics maintain.

Problem: Should stiffer penalties be inflicted on those who violate the drug, tax and traffic laws?

Arguments for

1. _____

2. _____

3. _____

Arguments against

1. _____

2. _____

3. _____

Questions: Is the problem as bad as stated above? What does it mean for a Christian to be responsible in regard to the law?

FOUR

The Ethical Teaching
of Jesus

To dream the impossible dream,
To fight the unbeatable foe,
To bear with unbearable sorrow,
To run where the brave dare not go.

To right the unrightable wrong,
To love, pure and chaste, from afar,
To try, when your arms are too weary,
To reach the unreachable star!

This is my quest . . .
　　　　　　　—from *Man of La Mancha*

The words quoted above come from the highly successful Broadway musical, later a movie, *Man of La Mancha.* The play tells the story of the famed fictional idealist, Don Quixote. Quixote is one of those rare individuals who meet the problems of life with a positive, self-sacrificing attitude of service for others. He inspires the audience because he is willing to meet the challenges of life head-on. He doesn't allow pessimism or negative attitudes to infect his thinking. As a result, he comes across as a Christ-figure who seems very relevant in a world where Christian virtue is often laughed at or ignored.

In some ways we Christians are like Quixote. Our Lord calls us to live a way of life which appears to many to be an impossible dream. But it is precisely in following Jesus that the impossible becomes possible. In this chapter we will investigate more closely the message and the ideal with which Jesus challenges each of us, his followers.

Before looking at this message, let us state quite emphatically that Christian morality flows from Jesus Christ. How seriously we take Jesus will affect how we react to his message.

Jesus is the message. We Christians believe that he is "the way, the truth, and the life." Following him brings happiness and meaning to our lives.

Let us begin this chapter by reflecting on the role Jesus currently plays in your life. Who is Jesus to you?

SOME REFLECTIONS

1. What is your *current* relationship with Jesus?
2. What are three of your major beliefs about Jesus Christ?
3. What do you admire most about Jesus and his story?
4. Has prayer to the Lord ever helped you?

Share: If you care to, share your responses to these questions with your classmates.

Your responses to the reflection questions above may help you answer Jesus' question: "Who do you say that I am?" Jesus asked this question of his apostles on the dusty roads of the Holy Land many years ago. But he wants you to answer the question for yourself today. Christians believe that he makes all the difference in the world; he is the one who can be all things to us. As Cardinal Newman wrote:

> Life passes, riches fly away, popularity is fickle, the senses decay, the world changes. One alone is true to us; One alone can be all things to us; One alone can supply our need.

Certainly in the area of morality what we believe about Jesus and what he said and did will make a difference in the way we act toward others. If he is indeed the Son of God who came to show us the way to his Father, then he is *the* crucial factor in helping us to discover what is right.

JESUS AS THE MESSAGE

The following quotation from St. John's first epistle shows keen insight into an important aspect of Christianity. It talks of love as the central reality for Christian life. This love flows from our true identity in Jesus Christ.

> Think of the love that the Father has lavished on us,
> by letting us be called God's children;
> and that is what we are.
> Because the world refused to acknowledge him,
> therefore it does not acknowledge us.
> My dear people, we are already the children of God
> but what we are to be in the future has not yet been
>   revealed;
> all we know is, that when it is revealed
> we shall be like him
> because we shall see him as he really is.
> Surely everyone who entertains this hope
> must purify himself, must try to be as pure as
>   Christ. . . .
> This has taught us love—
> that he gave up his life for us;
> and we, too, ought to give up our lives for our
>   brothers.
> If a man who was rich enough in this world's goods
> saw that one of his brothers was in need,
> but closed his heart to him,
> how could the love of God be living in him?
> My children,
> our love is not to be just words or mere talk,
> but something real and active (1 Jn 3:1-3,16-18).

As we have seen before, an essential Christian insight into the human condition is that we are the children of God and brothers and sisters of his Son, Jesus. We should live that reality of adopted children by loving others.

Jesus, our brother and Savior, provided the example. The mystery of the incarnation, God becoming one of us in the person of Jesus Christ, reveals what God wants of his children. Through the incarnation God the Father provided a profound lesson for us. His son humbled himself to become one with us. The great, almighty, infinite and all-knowing God joined himself to his creation in the person of a man. This profound act of self-giving love, of true humility, teaches us the true meaning of service and Christian love.

Through the humanity of Jesus, God the Father spoke to

us. Jesus' whole life, not only what he taught and spoke, but his every action—his miracles, his loving presence at meals and among the sick in pressing crowds, and especially his suffering, death and resurrection—speaks to us about fundamental reality.

For Jesus, reality was doing the will of his Father. He sums up in his very being the *really real*; he shows what it means to live, what it means to love. He taught us in human words and with human gestures that his Father intends us to be united to him. Jesus actually showed us the greatest form of human love—that of giving one's life for another, for us. Jesus' message was real. By dying on the cross he put into action the message he spent three years preaching.

One summary of Jesus' message can be found in the Sermon on the Mount. It is known as the Golden Rule: "Treat others as you would like them to treat you; that is the meaning of the Law and the Prophets" (Mt 7:12).

Do to others what you would have them do to you. This message is an action message; it requires positive effort on behalf of others. Contrast this with the teaching of a famous Jewish rabbi of Jesus' day: "Avoid doing to others what you do not wish them to do to you." The message of Jesus is to get involved as the Father has gotten involved with humanity; the rabbi wants us merely to keep from harming others. Jesus calls us to positive action, not just reaction.

My dear people,
let us love one another
since love comes from God
and everyone who loves is begotten by God and
    knows God.
Anyone who fails to love can never have known God,
because God is love.
God's love for us was revealed
when God sent into the world his only Son
so that we could have life through him;
this is the love I mean:
not our love for God,
but God's love for us when he sent his Son
to be the sacrifice that takes our sins away.
My dear people,
since God has loved us so much,
we too should love one another (1 Jn 4:7-11).

REACT OR ACT?

Here are some situations in which you might find yourself. Imagine what your response might be to each. Then decide if your way of handling the situation is one of positive action. Which items qualify as fulfilling Jesus' mandate to "treat others as you would like them to treat you"?

1. A classmate makes fun of another classmate who has a speech impediment.
2. A casual friend shoplifts while you are walking through a department store.
3. A bum asks you to give him money for bus fare.
4. Your school cafeteria has a litter problem.
5. You have a seat on a crowded bus. An old woman boards and has to stand. She looks directly at you.
6. Your parish makes an appeal for help in raising money for a drop-in center for runaway kids.
7. Your friend has a definite drinking problem.

Discuss: Share your responses. Would you consider it wrong not to do something to remedy the above situations? Why or why not?

THE LAW OF JESUS

As you shared responses to the last exercise you probably concluded that two people can be committed to action but can easily come up with two different solutions to the same problem. Wouldn't it be nice if we could turn to some source that would tell us what to do in the messy moral dilemmas of everyday life? Some people would even like to turn to the New Testament to find concrete answers to all of their moral problems.

But one of the major problems in discussing the moral teaching of Jesus is the difficulty in citing *rules* to cover every situation in which we might find ourselves. Jesus did not directly address abortion or euthanasia or nuclear weapons or many other pressing moral issues we have today.

In his day Jesus did two things: He addressed a few concrete moral issues which people brought to him; for example, the question of divorce and the question of whether one should pay taxes. More important, Jesus gave us his example of how we should do right and avoid wrong and, in addition, taught the important principles which his followers need to apply to concrete everyday human situations.

As St. John repeats time and again in his gospel and epistles, much of Christian morality revolves around love. For Jesus, love is the fundamental principle of morality; that is, the fundamental truth on which we should base our conduct. He demonstrated this principle by his actions. For Jesus, love was always rooted in the concrete life situation of interaction among real people. Luke's gospel, for example, records the story of the notorious woman who anointed Jesus' feet. Despite her many sins Jesus forgave her because she demonstrated great love. Indeed, she was even seen as more hospitable than the hypocritical Simon the Pharisee who had invited Jesus to dinner but failed to treat him with the courtesy due a guest.

Jesus' law of love often got him into trouble with the official interpretation of the Law. For example, he healed a chronically ill woman on the Sabbath. Our Lord considered his compassionate action more important than an interpretation of the Mosaic Law about how one should keep the Sabbath holy.

For Jesus, love is not a feeling to be swept away by or to sing about. Love expresses itself in freely-made decisions, in concrete human deeds like pardoning, lending money without expecting repayment, showing compassion and refraining from judging and condemning others.

THE OLD AND NEW LAWS

Read and discuss the following passages from the Bible. What is the essential difference between them?

Deuteronomy 5:1-22   Matthew 5:17-48

Now read Romans 13:9-10. What is the main point Paul is making?

THE PARADOX IN JESUS' TEACHING

The more closely we look at the moral teaching of Jesus, the more we begin to notice its paradoxical nature. (A *paradox* is a statement which appears to contradict itself.) Let us consider a few examples.

"You know that among the pagans their so-called rulers lord it over them, and their great men make their authority felt. This is not to happen among you. No; anyone who wants to become great among you must be your servant, and anyone who wants to be first among you must be slave to all. For the Son of Man himself did not come to be served but to serve, and to give his life as a ransom for many" (Mk 10:43-45).

By the standards of today's world, this code of living seems ridiculous. The world would ask: How can you be great and powerful if you go around serving others? But for Jesus, and the Christian who imitates him, true greatness lies in serving others, not being served by them.

In John's gospel this same teaching appears when Jesus goes around and washes the feet of the apostles. This action of Jesus occurred after a dispute among the disciples as to which one would sit at the place of honor in the kingdom he would establish. Here, in their last moments with Jesus, the apostles were arguing over a place of importance. They seemed to miss the whole thrust of what he had been teaching in his three years with them.

To teach them that places of honor and that greatness in the eyes of the world were not part of his message, Jesus got up from his place at the head of the table and washed their feet. This task was very humiliating and reserved only for the servant or the slave. Jesus performed it to indicate the wisdom of his paradoxical saying that the first shall be last, and the last first. In a way, every Christian is a foot washer, a person who serves others without thinking about self.

FOR REFLECTION

A. Every Christian is a foot washer. Discuss the implications of this paradox for

- a student council leader
- a parent
- the president of the United States
- the head of a small business
- a doctor
- a city worker

B. What does it mean for you "to wash feet?" How do you serve others? Give a couple of examples of how you have served in the past few months or so

- at home
- at school
- among your friends
- for anyone you have been with on a daily basis

Jesus also presented a paradox to the Pharisee Nicodemus when he told Nicodemus that he had to be born again in order to live. Jesus was, of course, talking about death to sin and about spiritual rebirth through faith in him and baptism.

Behind this teaching of Jesus stands the paradox that to live a person must die to self. This saying makes little sense when measured against the standards of the world. These standards often tell us to indulge and gorge ourselves on the goods of the world. They rarely, if ever, tell us to deny ourselves, to die to self.

But Jesus' teaching about self-sacrifice makes sense. To the degree that we die to self, we love. And it is by loving that we find true life. We can only love when we give up our self-interest (die to self) and go out to others. But when we go out to another, that is, when we love, we become more of who we are; we really live.

Love is the one "commodity" that the more we "spend" the more we have. We know this not only from our own experience, but also because Jesus made this promise:

"I tell you solemnly, there is no one who has left house, brothers, sisters, father, children or land for my sake and for the sake of the gospel who will not be repaid a hundred times over, houses, brothers, sisters, mothers, children and land—not without persecutions—now in this present time and, in the world to come, eternal life.

"Many who are first will be last, and the last first" (Mk 10:28-31).

EXERCISES

A. *Interview:* Ask your parents how they see their marriage as a way of Christian service. Share their insights with your classmates.

B. *Career Choice:*

1. At this point in your life, what would you like to do to earn a living?

2. Name several ways that you can serve others in this career.

3. Interview someone who has the kind of job you would like to have. Find out how this person is serving others.

THE SERMON ON THE MOUNT

More than any other place in the New Testament, the moral teaching of Jesus is best summarized in Matthew 5-7, the famed Sermon on the Mount. Every Christian should read and study it often. It is to the New Testament what the Ten Commandments are to the Old Testament.

Please read the Sermon on the Mount, Matthew 5-7, now.

The Sermon is addressed to those who want to follow Jesus, to those who have accepted the good news of God's love and have made a basic conversion, a turning to Jesus. This conversion is a lifelong process. We Christians are weak and subject to sin, but our fundamental direction is to Christ; his grace continually pulls us toward him.

The Sermon on the Mount captures the joyfulness of the person who makes a basic decision for Jesus Christ. It begins with the Beatitudes, which proclaim a new order for those who hunger and thirst for God. Our hunger and thirst will be satisfied by Jesus—and beyond our expectations. Jesus concludes the Beatitudes with this joyful note: "Rejoice and be glad, for your reward will be great in heaven" (Mt 5:12). One who accepts Jesus and his teaching has every right to rejoice for having found the truth.

The next section of the Sermon briefly discusses the Christian as the salt of the earth and the light of the world. (These two images will be treated in some detail in Chapter 10 of this book.) Matthew then mentions that Jesus has come to fulfill the Old Law, not to overthrow it. This point is elaborated in the next verses by a comparison of the teaching of Moses with the new, fuller teaching of Jesus in moral matters. Note how Jesus intensifies the Old Law by setting a higher standard for his followers:

Old Law	New Law
a. You must not kill, and if you do, settle at court.	a. You must not even be angry with one another. And if you are, settle your dispute before worshiping.
b. You must not commit adultery.	b. If you even look lustfully on another, you have committed adultery in your thoughts.
c. If you divorce, give your wife a writ of divorce.	c. You must not divorce.
d. You must not break your oath.	d. There is no need for oaths because a Christian always says what he or she means.
e. "Eye for eye and tooth for tooth."	e. Offer the wicked no resistance; turn the other cheek; give of your cloak; walk an extra mile.
f. Love your neighbor, but hate your enemy.	f. Love your enemies and pray for those who persecute you.

These six teachings show the intense kind of love Jesus requires of his followers. It is the kind of love he himself showed to his disciples day in and day out. It is the kind of love that led him to Calvary where he offered up his life so that all of us could achieve eternal salvation.

In other sections of the Sermon Jesus calls for purity of intention. He asks that money be given to the poor without a show of generosity to impress others. He requests that prayers be recited simply, and gives us the perfect Christian prayer, the Our Father. When we fast, Jesus does not want us to advertise the fact that we are doing penance. The point is that Jesus wants us to do good works, but not in a way that shows off. He requires that we be satisfied with the knowledge that God our Father sees and blesses our good works and our prayers.

The Sermon on the Mount is a challenge to Christians today. Many of us do not know how we should take what Jesus taught. Does he really mean that we should "offer no resistance to injury"? Or is he speaking in an exaggerated way to get us to see the importance of loving? Christians for centuries have been wrestling with how literally we should take the directives of the Sermon on the Mount.

A Catholic interpretation of the Sermon current among moral theologians is that the teachings in the Sermon are *directional norms,* norms that point to the kind of life we Christians must live if we wish to be identified with Jesus. Every Christian must take them very seriously and try, with God's loving grace, to live up to them. What is needed is continuous conversion—a deepening relationship with Jesus whereby we can better live the words of life that Jesus has given to us.

Such an interpretation of the Sermon on the Mount should make us uncomfortable; to be Christian means to live in tension. This is a healthy tension which prompts us to be concerned about and involved with our brothers and sisters. It prompts us always to try to do more. And, if we try to implement these goals in our own lives, we are promised a sense of peace which comes from the Spirit of Jesus. What greater good can there be?

ANOTHER INTERPRETATION

Another view of the Sermon on the Mount is that Jesus meant it as an ethics of the kingdom of God. In other words, for those who have been given the good news of God's love, the Lord asks that they in fact live this higher code of morality. In this view, the Sermon does not provide an ideal toward which we strive; rather, it gives a standard which the Lord *commands* us to live. If we fail, then we should accuse ourselves of sin and ask for God's forgiveness.

Discuss:

1. Which interpretation of the Sermon on the Mount makes more sense to you? Why?

2. Can a Christian ignore the various sayings in the Sermon and still be considered a Christian? Explain.

3. A pacifist is, in principle, against participation in all war. Which interpretation of the Sermon on the Mount discussed above would a pacifist probably support? Why?

OTHER NEW TESTAMENT TEACHINGS

The Sermon on the Mount gives us a good notion of Jesus' ideas on morality. The New Testament also reveals these other five general directions for Christian living:

1. We should keep material goods in their proper perspective. We should not be enslaved by them; rather, they should serve us.

2. We should be relative pacifists, that is, we should with the greatest of energy try to solve our problems with others in a peaceful way. As Jesus himself states, "All who draw the sword will die by the sword" (Mt 26:52).

3. To follow Christ, to walk in his footsteps, means we have to be willing to suffer. Any goal worth striving for is worth suffering for, is worth denying ourselves for. Redemption and healing come through suffering.

4. Others, even our families, must not block our progress in spiritual matters. Nothing can get in the way of our following Christ.

5. In the way we pray, in the way we do good works, in the way we serve others, our attitude should be one of humility. We should be content with the thought that God the Father knows and appreciates the good that we do and not seek praise from others.

CHRISTIAN MORALITY IN PRACTICE

1. Read Luke 10:29-37, the parable of the Good Samaritan.
    a. With whose actions and motives do you most closely identify—the priest? the Levite? the Samaritan? Why?
    b. Could you think of some circumstances that might serve as a good reason for the priest or Levite not to get involved? Explain.

2. How would you respond to these situations?
    a. You notice a classmate eating lunch alone almost every day.
    b. You witness two "toughs" harassing an old "wino" on a bus.
    c. You read in the paper that a poor family in your city is in need of food, shelter and clothing.
    d. When filling out your income tax return, you notice that the government is asking for a contribution from the taxpayers to help reduce the public debt.

Discuss:
    1. Could you justify your responses in light of the Sermon on the Mount? Why or why not?
    2. Would you have a greater responsibility to get involved in the first two situations? Explain.

THE TEN COMMANDMENTS

In light of Jesus' moral teaching the ethical wisdom of the Old Testament is seen in its full glory. The Old Testament summary of our response to God is, of course, the Ten Commandments. These commandments are fully understood only in the context of covenant.

The ancient Israelites understood their relationship to Yahweh in terms of covenant. A covenant implied certain rights and duties. God specially blessed the Jewish people. He delivered them from Egypt, gave them a land and nationhood. In brief, he created them as a people and sustained them through his abundant blessings whenever they were undergoing trials, hardships, sufferings and persecutions. Indeed, he sustained them despite their unfaithfulness.

For their part, the Jews were to live a certain quality of life which would help them maintain their identity as God's Chosen People and help them be a sign to all nations of the oneness, majesty and glory of their God—the one true God. In sum, the Jews were to live the Law, summarized in the Ten Commandments, as an affirmation of Yahweh's gracious calling and his act of creating them as his chosen people.

Today we live the Ten Commandments, not as a burdensome list of obligations, but as a willing response to God's loving call to be his people. By living the Ten Commandments we say yes to our identity, to our vocation. This vocation is to witness in the Spirit to the Father of Jesus the Lord. In studying the Ten Commandments, try to focus on how each is a *response* in love to a loving God. (The version of the commandments given below is from Deuteronomy 5:6-21).

The first three commandments focus on our response to God and emphasize our need to love God above all things.

1. **"I am Yahweh your God who brought you out of the land of Egypt, out of the house of slavery. You shall have no gods except me."**

   This commandment stresses the need to set priorities. Our problem today is not that we worship golden calves, but that we make good things more important than their Creator. Sex, money, power, prestige are all good in their place, but when we make our whole life revolve around them we no longer have things in proper perspective. We are unfaithful to God when we substitute one of these other things for him.

2. **"You shall not utter the name of Yahweh your God to misuse it, for Yahweh will not leave unpunished the man who utters his name to misuse it."**

   The second commandment emphasizes that some things are sacred. Our speech reflects who we are. A respectful attitude to God's holiness shows that we are creatures and that God is our Creator. This commandment also applies to the way we worship God. Our attitude should be one of confident humility, asking that God's will be done. We should not demand that God do our will.

3. **"Observe the sabbath day and keep it holy, as Yahweh your God has commanded you."**

   Faithfulness to God demands that we adore him. It is his will that we do so with others. Our salvation is not something we work at alone. We in the Christian community realize the extreme importance of presenting ourselves to the Father joined to our Lord with our fellow Christians in the Holy Spirit. Sunday, the day of the Lord's resurrection, is a day to set priorities.

   The last seven commandments focus on our response to God through others and point to our obligation to love our neighbor as ourselves.

4. **"Honor your father and your mother."**

   Covenant love extends to our families. Children owe their parents love; they show love to parents through respect, obedience, courtesy and gratitude. Parents, too, have an obligation to love their children by caring for them, educating them and respecting their dignity as individuals.

Finally, brothers and sisters owe each other courtesy, respect, patience and kindness. Christian family love can then be a sign of God's love at work in the world.

5. "You shall not kill."

This commandment underscores the importance of respecting the gift of life God has given to us. We have a serious obligation to watch out for the life and safety of others; for example, by curbing reckless behavior such as bad driving. We must also care for our own bodies. We do this by eating good food, avoiding harmful substances such as drugs, and getting proper rest and relaxation. We must, in addition, work to protect innocent life—the old, the chronically sick, the poor and the unborn.

6. "You shall not commit adultery."

Unfaithfulness to the marriage covenant—adultery—is unfaithfulness to the covenant of unity to which God calls each married couple. Likewise, an improper use of our procreative faculties distorts the divine plan of creative love. Responsible use of sex shows deep concern for others and their dignity.

7. "You shall not steal."

Theft destroys trust. Trust is needed for smooth human relationships. Shoplifting and cheating are two widespread forms of stealing in today's world; they both destroy trust.

8. "You shall not bear false witness against your neighbor."

Revenge, gossip, scandal and lies all destroy love. The tongue can be a cruel weapon that cuts as sharply as a knife. Further, honesty is the touchstone of one's character. Lies and deceit distort the mission of the Christian who is called to witness to the truth which sets us free.

9. "You shall not covet your neighbor's wife."

and

10. "You shall not set your heart on . . . anything that is his."

Obsessive desire and lust which can grow out of jealousy, materialism or selfishness destroy love between neighbors and friends. Internal desires can breed hatred and rivalry. These two commandments show the importance of pure intentions and decent motives when dealing with others. They demonstrate that destruction of relationships comes from within.

RECAP

The ethical teachings of Jesus make sense if we accept the fundamental reality that Jesus is God. He has shown us the best way to live as human beings. To live the Christian moral ethic means to let Jesus live in us. He has promised his Spirit to those who believe in him. This gift of the Holy Spirit gives us the strength to do the work of our Lord in the world today. In a very real way, he depends on us to do that work—we are his hands, his feet, his loving touch present to others.

Much of Christian morality makes sense in the context of our concept of the human person. Jesus' ethical demands boil down to "Be who you are." We are sons and daughters of God our Father and brothers and sisters to our Savior Jesus Christ. We should live like the family we are, united intimately to the Lord. The church—which is the family of believers, God's people—has the duty to show others the way.

SUMMARY

1. What we believe about Jesus will make a difference in the way we act toward others.

2. Jesus' actions and teachings show us how love should express itself in our dealings with others.

3. Jesus taught the important principles for living our Christian commitment. We can find these principles in the New Testament, especially in the Sermon on the Mount.

4. Jesus' moral teaching is paradoxical; for example, it instructs us that the way to honor in God's kingdom is to serve others.

5. Love demands self-sacrifice, a kind of dying to our own self-interest.

6. Christian moral response demands continuous conversion, a deepening relationship with the Lord so that we may each day try to be better than we were in the past.

7. The Ten Commandments show us the way of responding to God's covenant love with his people. They show us how to love God and neighbor.

ACTIVITIES

A. *Gospel Search*: Divide into four groups. Each group is to investigate one of the gospels and come up with some moral teachings of Jesus not discussed in this chapter. Discuss these questions:

1. In what way do these teachings focus on people rather than on just obeying a list of rules?

2. How might these teachings be applied today:
   a. in your school
   b. in your home
   c. by our government

B. *Proclaiming Jesus*: Imagine that you were transported to another world where people had never heard about Jesus or his teaching. If you were allowed to preach to those people only three of Jesus' teachings about morality, what would they be?

Compare your choices with those of your classmates and arrive at a consensus on the three most important moral teachings of Jesus.

C. *Case for Discussion*

Some time ago a professional boxer died of head injuries received in a match. Soon after the incident there was a predictable outcry to ban boxing. Some people claim that any sport that has as its purpose rendering an opponent unconscious is barbaric and thus wrong.

Discuss the following:

1. After studying the ethical teaching of Jesus, what would you say about the morality of boxing?

2. If you decided that boxing is wrong, what would you say about other sports that tend to hurt people, for example, hockey or football?

D. Can sports in general be a very good thing? Why or why not? What can make them bad? How do questions of morality fit into the following issues?

1. The ridiculously high salaries of some professional athletes.

2. The overemphasis on sports in some of our high schools.

3. Gambling on the outcome of sports events.

FIVE

Conscience

Conscience is condensed character.
—Anonymous

Children are familiar with the story of Jiminy Cricket who tells Pinocchio always to let his conscience be his guide. The wisdom of this advice hits people as they grow older. But many are also painfully aware of the problem presented by this advice: What is your conscience?

Conscience is sometimes called the subjective norm of morality. This means that conscience arises from within us and helps us make moral decisions. Our conscience helps us take into consideration all the available data when confronted with a decision. It aids us in making the final judgment to act or not to act in a given situation. Along with the objective norm of morality—law—conscience helps us to determine whether we are doing right or wrong. This chapter will try to define and describe conscience, and the next chapter will discuss the role of law.

CALLS FOR CONSCIENCE

Presented below are several situations which call for a conscience response. Please read and study each of the situations and decide how you would resolve the problems.

Situation A:

You go to a school where there is a lot of pressure to achieve high grades. Your parents also expect you to do well. You are carrying a *B* average and are now in your senior year. Your sociology teacher is not the best in the school and, as a matter of fact, is a bit unfair. He has planned a difficult test for you and your classmates. You know from past experience that 50 percent of the students cheat on his exams. You have studied pretty hard, but you know that unless you cheat, many others will get a higher grade than you. What would you do?

Reasons for cheating:

1. _____

2. _____

3. _____

4. _____

Reasons for honesty:

1. _____

2. _____

3. _____

4. _____

My decision: On a scale from *1* (most inclined to cheat) to *5* (I will remain honest), I would decide:

☐   ☐   ☐   ☐   ☐
1   2   3   4   5

Situation B:

Your good friend offers you a drug. At first you refuse her offer. She tries to talk you into it by saying that she has only experienced fun with drugs. "Besides," she says, "you can't really hurt anyone but yourself." She adds that it is nobody's business but yours whether you take drugs or not. The law and parents should not prevent you from enjoying yourself. Would you take the drug?

Reasons for taking it:

1. _____

2. _____

3. _____

4. _____

Reasons for not taking it:

1. _____

2. _____

3. _____

4. _____

My decision: On a scale of *1* (most inclined to take it) to *5* (I will not take the drug), I would decide:

☐   ☐   ☐   ☐   ☐
1   2   3   4   5

Situation C:

After high school you enter the Air Force. Your country is at war with a small nation which may go communist. You respect law and believe very much in the values of your own country. On a particular day you are ordered to participate in a secret mission. You and your crew are to bomb and totally destroy a small village. The village is *suspected* of containing a pocket of terrorists, but it is *known* that many old people and small children who are not participants in the war live in the village. Should you bomb?

Reasons to bomb:	*Reasons not to bomb:*
1. _____	1. _____
2. _____	2. _____
3. _____	3. _____
4. _____	4. _____

My decision: On a scale from *1* (most inclined to obey the order) to *5* (I refuse to obey the command), I would decide:

☐   ☐   ☐   ☐   ☐
1   2   3   4   5

WHAT IS CONSCIENCE?

It is important to know what conscience is in order to respond better to others and to God. Conscience is often described as an inner voice which tells us what is right and what is wrong.

Perhaps a better way to describe conscience is in terms of self-awareness. Conscience enables us to be aware of ourselves and helps us act so that we become the persons we are capable of becoming. In other words, conscience is the *capacity to judge* whether an action or an attitude will help us grow as persons or whether such actions and attitudes will stifle, even kill, our growth as children of God.

As Christians, we know that our growth or non-growth does not take place in a vacuum. Our actions and attitudes involve others as well as ourselves. A religious notion of conscience sees it this way: *Conscience is our inner dialogue with God who calls each one of us to act as the person we are.* It is a judgment in the inner core of our being. This judgment helps us become what we are meant to become. If our conscience is formed properly, and if we decide to abide by its dictates, it helps us to respond to God's invitation to live as his children.

A properly formed conscience, then, helps tune us in to what God wants for us in a particular situation. It comes into play at three separate points in every decision and action. Here is an example:

> Bob used the family car last night. While backing out of the parking lot on his way home, he damaged another car to the tune of about $300. He did about $100 worth of damage to the family car. Realizing that his insurance rates would skyrocket if he admitted the accident, Bob did not leave a note on the damaged car, nor did he try to locate its owner. Today Bob feels uneasy over his decision.

Bob's conscience was at work:

a. *Before he acted,* when he was trying to judge what to do or what not to do. Conscience helps a person to sort the data before a decision is made. It prompts us to look at the alternatives involved and the various consequences of each alternative. It helps in examining the right or wrong thing to do by reflecting on the teaching of our Lord and his church, the rights of others and the helpfulness to our growth.

b. *As he acted,* by enabling him to make a judgment after considering the relevant data. Conscience ultimately makes it possible for a person to act or not to act, to hold an attitude or not to hold one. It is that depth of our being which says "Yes, I am going to act," or "No, I refuse to act."

c. *After he acted,* through any afterthoughts he may have about his action the previous night. The third function of conscience is to help a person judge after the action whether the initial judgment was right. In Bob's case maybe fear the night before blinded him to the right thing to do. If he is "conscientious" today, he will regret his action and try to make amends.

Before leaving Bob's case, note two important points: First, *our conscience can be misinformed.* We may do the wrong thing because we have wrong information or no information at all. Sometimes we are at fault for either having wrong information or for our lack of knowledge. At other times, we are not at fault. Our obligation is to keep an open mind and to positively seek out the truth. Misinformation was not part of Bob's case.

Second, *we can violate our conscience.* Bob's conscience may very well have told him what to do before he acted (the first step above), but he simply may have ignored it. When we choose what our conscience clearly tells us is wrong, we do the wrong thing, we sin.

CONSCIENCE SURVEY

Below are three statements representing different ways of looking at conscience. Please mark the scale provided from *5* (strongly agree with the statement) to *1* (strongly disagree).

1. Something is right for me if I think it is right.

    ☐   ☐   ☐   ☐   ☐
    5   4   3   2   1

2. In making moral decisions, sincerity is all that matters.

    ☐   ☐   ☐   ☐   ☐
    5   4   3   2   1

3. No one has the right to judge my actions right or wrong.

    ☐   ☐   ☐   ☐   ☐
    5   4   3   2   1

Discuss in small groups:

a. If sincerity is what matters, then was it all right for Hitler to kill the Jews? for war resisters to burn draft board records? Is it OK for you to steal from a store to give money to the poor? Give reasons for your answers to each of these questions.

b. If some action is right because "I think it is right," what role does law have? Do other people play any part at all in our moral decisions? Explain.

Sincerity and Freedom

Though Catholic Christians believe that sincerity and personal freedom are important in making conscience decisions, they are not supreme. For the Christian, individual decisions are always made with others in mind. For example, in the case of the car accident (see page 80), it is very important for Bob *sincerely* to arrive at a decision and to do so *freely*. But his sincerity and freedom do not make his action right! He must also take into consideration the rights of the owner of the damaged car. Further, he should consider the consequences of his action for society as a whole. What if everyone were dishonest in dealings with others? Society could hardly exist. And without a society which judges behavior as sometimes good and sometimes bad, Bob would not even have the right/privilege to drive in the first place.

Sincerity must always be tempered with correct judgment. And correct judgment should be in accord with the natural law and God's will as made known to us in divine revelation. For ex-

ample, we Catholics believe that neither good intentions nor a good outcome justify bad actions. Just because Bob wanted lower insurance rates (a good intention/good outcome) does not mean that he was justified in leaving the scene of an accident (a bad action). This principle, a key one in Catholic morality, is sometimes stated this way: *The end does not justify the means.*

IMPLICATIONS

Discuss the implications for society if good intentions were allowed to justify these actions:

- abortion (to protect a person's good reputation)
- theft (in order to feed the poor)
- getting drunk (in order to relax from the tensions of job or school)
- killing (in order to end a person's pain)
- forced sterilization (to limit overpopulation)

Thought question: Suppose your conscience comes into conflict with either church teaching or with the law of society. Should you first question church teaching and the law or your own conscience? Why?

An Important Influence

Peer relationships play an important role in shaping our values, especially during the adolescent years. Friends are vital to making moral decisions. But the advice of friends must not be our sole consideration in choosing the right thing to do. As with sincerity, the advice of our friends must always be tempered with correct judgment. We must know and act on our own values. To follow blindly the will of another is not to be a friend, but to be a mindless puppet. True friendship respects differences and helps each partner to feel more secure with his or her own convictions. Jesus' warning that if the blind lead the blind, both will fall into the ditch, makes tremendous sense when applied to matters of conscience.

KINDS OF CONSCIENCE

Consider this case:

Tom, Sally and Jack were with their friends the other evening celebrating the end of the school year. They were coming back from a party when one of the members of the group suggested that it would be great fun to drive onto the fairways of a suburban country club and tear up one of the greens. Several members of the group decided to engage in the destruction, but Tom, Sally and Jack decided not to do so.

By investigating the reasons the three friends did not engage in "The Case of the Torn-up Greens," we can discover three basic types of conscience.

Type 1: *"Fear" Conscience or "What Am I Going to Get Out of It?"*

Tom arrived at his decision not to join in the destruction for one simple reason—he was afraid he might be caught. He really wanted to be with the others, but his fear of the law kept him from doing so. Tom is like those who see God, church, parents and all authority figures as "cops" who are out to punish people for slipping up. In their better moments, they also see authority figures as those who will reward them for being good. They conform not so much because it is the right thing to do, but because they fear the bad consequences of their actions or look forward to the external rewards that will be theirs for doing the right thing.

Type 2: *"A Need to Please" Conscience*

Sally also declined the invitation to joyride, but her reasoning was an advance on Tom's. Her conscience easily detected the folly of destroying someone else's property. She realized that by engaging in this action other people would be hurt. Sally appreciates the fact that a mature person tries to please others and works to respect the laws that help keep society together. She is more sensitive than Tom who seems more concerned with his own interests than with pleasing others or respecting the law.

Type 3: *Christian Conscience*

Jack demonstrated a high level of conscience development. Like Sally, he was concerned about others and also with the role of law. But his motivation was different. He considered the teaching of Jesus and saw the owners of the golf course as his own brothers and sisters in the Lord. He responded to the Spirit's call to treat everyone with love, to "treat others as you would have them treat you." His criterion for choosing the right thing was neither fear nor expectation of reward; it was not merely to please others or to uphold a no-trespassing law. Jack clearly sees the real purpose of the law—to protect the property rights of other human beings who are our equals. He views the matter in terms of true justice and in terms of a love response to Jesus. His conscience dictates that he should respond to others in a sensitive, caring way.

Tom, Sally and Jack all did the right thing, even though they may have had different motives. They should all be praised for their good actions. However, the goal of Christian conscience formation is to get beyond fear as a motivation for action.

Responding to people as persons related to us as brothers and sisters in Christ is the ideal in Christian behavior. Living our lives as children of God with a destiny of final union with him is the norm of Christian living. And the conscience that prompts us to act in this way is the mature conscience.

CONSCIENCE FORMATION

Jack's case, the Christian conscience, clearly demonstrates our obligations in regard to conscience:

1. We must follow our conscience.

2. We must develop an informed conscience.

But how do we form this Type 3 conscience? How do we make decisions based on conscience?

Here is a helpful check list compiled from the *National Catechetical Directory* and from the work of author Father

Gerard Sloyan. It lists several points which can help in the development of an informed conscience, one which leads to correct moral decisions.

- *Have a pure intention.* Sincerity is important. If we want to do something simply to get away with it, we hardly have a pure intention. The following questions help determine intentions: Why do I want to do this? Is my motive selfish? Is it for the sake of others? Will this action benefit me, that is, help me grow? Have I considered all the data, or am I acting on impulse?

- *Consult the teaching of Jesus in the New Testament, the prophets, Moses and Paul.* If we really want to be followers of Jesus Christ, then we must know what he said and seriously reflect on its meaning as best we can. Am I aware, for example, of the ethical teachings of Jesus? the Ten Commandments? the position of the church? Scripture helps us discern God's will for us. It contains the specifics of Christian morality in the Beatitudes, the Sermon on the Mount, the commandments and other teachings which help us respond to the Lord in loving ways.

- *Ask the question: How does this action measure up to the yardstick of love?* For Christians, every authentic response to God and neighbor is a response in love. And love is not something watered down, but a real self-sacrificing attempt to meet God and others.

- *Consult the people of God, the church, which is the Body of Christ and which has been promised the Holy Spirit.* We must investigate the teaching and belief of theologians, holy and learned Christians, the brotherhood and sisterhood of believers. Do I care what church teaching is? Do I consult it? Do I bother asking other Christians for an opinion? Do I give special weight to the teachings of the pope and the bishops who have been anointed by the Holy Spirit to be the official and authentic teachers of the Christian life?

- *Follow the current debate on great moral issues.* What are my duties to the poor? How can I be just to those less fortunate? What are the pros and cons on the pressing life issues of today: abortion, euthanasia, fetal research, capital punishment, nuclear proliferation? What about sexual morality and issues of honesty? Especially, what is the position of the Catholic community on these issues?

- *Pray for God's guidance.* Have I asked God's Spirit to make me a creature of love? Our Lord God will not mislead us if we sincerely want to do the right thing and ask for his help. He will prompt us through other people, through insights, through the teachings of the church, and the like. And he will send us a peacefulness, a sense of knowing that we have done the right thing.

- *Acknowledge my own sinfulness and be sorrowful for my sins. Be humble and take advantage of the sacrament of reconciliation, recognizing that I need God's help.* There are times when we fail. At times we forget that we are God's children. There are those occasions when immediate gratification, when what others think, when laziness help influence us to make a wrong decision. But God understands our human condition. He simply wants us to admit that we have failed and that we need his help. Like the father in the parable of the Prodigal Son, our Lord is always willing to claim us as his own and shower his abundant love on us. All we need do is turn back to him and ask for his help.

- *Follow my conscience.* When all is said and done, have I followed my conscience?

REFLECTION

It would be a rare person indeed who considers all the above points in coming to a decision. They are, however, the goals toward which we strive in trying to develop informed consciences.

Read and study the list again. Think of an important decision you have made recently and see how many of the points above helped you in your decision.

The *National Catechetical Directory* sums up the process of responsible conscience development this way:

> We live in good faith if we act in accord with conscience. Nevertheless moral decisions still require much effort. Decisions of conscience must be based on prayer, study, consultation, and an understanding of the teachings of the Church. One must have a rightly formed conscience and follow it. But one's judgments are human and can be mistaken; one may be blinded by the power of sin or misled by the strength of desire. "Beloved, do not trust every spirit, but put the spirits to the test to see if they belong to God" (1 Jn 4:1; cf. 1 Cor 12:10).

Our obligation, then, is twofold: *We must develop an informed conscience,* and *we must follow that conscience.*

THE CASE OF THE GOSSIP

Slander is the uttering of a false charge which damages the reputation of another. Suppose you overhear a classmate slander another classmate. You don't know either of the individuals very well, but you do know that the classmate with the sharp tongue is lying and spreading false rumors.

Discuss: What would you do? What should you do? How might the points given in the check list on pages 86-87 help you arrive at a decision?

Would it matter? What if you knew the damaging remarks were in fact *true?* Would that change the situation? Why or why not?

SUMMARY

1. Conscience is the subjective norm of morality which enables us to make moral decisions.

2. Conscience is the capacity to judge the rightness or wrongness of our actions and attitudes. It is inner dialogue with the Lord who calls us to be what we are meant to be.

3. Conscience operates before, during and after our decisions. It is possible, however, to have a misinformed conscience or an ignorant one. We can also freely violate the dictates of our consciences. When we do, we are doing the wrong thing and are guilty of sin.

4. Sincerity is important, but it is not enough. It must be tempered with good judgment.

5. Friends strongly influence our attitudes and values. Their example and advice often carry weight with us in moral decision-making. Like sincerity, however, our friends' opinions must be tempered with our own good judgment.

6. A solid principle of Catholic morality is that the end does not justify the means. A good intention or reason for doing something does not justify using an evil way to achieve our purpose.

7. Conscience can operate out of motives of fear or expectation of reward, to please someone, or to uphold the law. It can also operate out of the highest principles of love and justice, recognizing the worth of others as children of God. Christians are called to judge issues in loving ways.

8. Christians have two obligations in dealing with conscience:

    a. Follow your conscience.

    b. Develop an informed conscience (a lifelong process).

SIMULATION: Jury

Scenario: The following simulation casts you as a member of a jury which is to decide what kinds of crimes and sins are most reprehensible, that is, outrageous to you and your fellow jurors.

Part 1:

1. On the following pages, 12 situations are described; all are potentially destructive of human relationships. After each situation is a key word which will help you remember the details of the story.

2. After reading each story, write the key word in the column entitled *Key Words* on page 93. Mark in the space to the right a number from *1* to *7* to measure your *emotional* reaction to each situation. (*1* represents the weakest emotional reaction; *7* the strongest.) You may use the same number as often as you like. You may change your reactions as you go along. But remember, measure your *emotional* reaction.

3. After you have read and reacted to all the situations in turn, rank the four which evoked your strongest emotional response, and the two which brought your weakest reaction. Write the key words in *Column E*.

Situation #1. A religion teacher at your school, married and the father of five children, was picked up last week by the police. Apparently he had accepted the solicitation of a "lady of the evening" and was about to take her to a motel room when they were caught by two members of a vice squad. TEACHER

Situation #2. A little boy, a neighborhood pest and brat, hates a certain old lady in the neighborhood who constantly yells at him for playing on her lawn. To get even with her, he fills a milk bottle with urine, props it against her front door and rings the doorbell. When she opens the door, the bottle falls into her living room soiling the rug. BOTTLE

Situation #3. The woman in the previous story seeks revenge on the neighborhood brat. On Halloween she inserts a razor blade into a shiny apple and gives it to the boy when he comes to the door. Later the boy bites into the apple and cuts his mouth rather badly. RAZOR BLADE

Situation #4. A prominent news item in the Sunday paper reveals that the American government is involved in supporting a Latin American regime which has been found guilty of assassinating missionaries working with the poor peasants on the issue of land reform. MISSIONARIES

Situation #5. A close friend confides to you that he stayed home from school the other day. He disguised his voice and called in sick by claiming he was his father. Since both of his parents were at work, he was free to use the family car. He did so and tells you he was involved in a near-fatal hit-and-run accident. Thus far neither the police nor his parents know of the crime. ACCIDENT

Situation #6. A TV news item reveals that high-placed government officials have been accepting bribes from a foreign nation which is trying to get favorable trade relations with this country. TRADE

Situation #7. The following situation is described to you by a close friend. On his annual Easter jaunt to Florida, your friend and his companion intended to play golf at a posh country club. When your friend went to pay his greens fee, he was told that the course was semiprivate. What this really meant was that he could not play because he was black. FRIEND

Situation #8. A neighbor girl who is in the third grade came home from school yesterday and told the family that her teacher, a man, kept her after school and, once they were alone, made sexual advances. NEIGHBOR GIRL.

Situation #9. The owner of a large industrial chemical plant is losing money by using his antipollution equipment. So, he opens the pollution control valves at night when no one is watching and allows the liquid pollutants to flow into a nearby stream. POLLUTANTS

Situation #10. A drunken motorist fell asleep at the wheel yesterday, lost control of her car, and caused an accident when the car ran up on the sidewalk injuring, luckily not killing, two passers-by. DRUNK

Situation #11. You have just purchased the car for which you have personally saved for a number of years. Before you can insure it, it is maliciously vandalized. CAR

Situation #12. A widow and her two young children have just returned from the funeral of her husband and their father to discover that some hoodlums have broken into their home and stolen most of their prized possessions. WIDOW

Part 2:

1. Form into small groups of six.

2. Compare your initial rankings.

3. Now, as a group re-rank the top four and bottom two. However, this time try to remove all emotion from your consideration. Judge on a rational basis alone. In other words, on the basis of reason, which of these situations evokes the strongest response? the weakest? Recopy these key words in *Column R*. (Your group should arrive at a consensus in about 15 minutes.)

Key Words   **Column E**

1. _____ ___   1. _____

2. _____ ___   2. _____

3. _____ ___   3. _____

4. _____ ___   4. _____

5. _____ ___   11. _____

6. _____ ___   12. _____

7. _____ ___   **Column R**

8. _____ ___   1. _____

9. _____ ___   2. _____

10. _____ ___   3. _____

11. _____ ___   4. _____

12. _____ ___   11. _____

                               12. _____

Part 3:

1. Gather in one large group.

2. One person from each of the small groups should share his or her group's rankings from *Column R* with the rest of the class. Give a brief statement of the reasons for the choices.

3. After each group has reported, discuss the following:

   a. Did your small group come to any different conclusions using reason than you did using emotion? If so, why? If not, why not?

   b. Was ranking by reason alone difficult? Is it difficult for a human being to judge any situation without emotional consideration?

   c. What made one situation more serious than another? (the number of people? the kind of people? the kind of crime? the role of the individual? etc.)

   d. What priorities did your group set in coming to consensus? Were they different from those of another group?

   e. How much did the intention of the characters in the stories affect your decisions? the circumstances? the action itself?

   f. What assumptions did you make about each story? Did these change any of your choices?

   g. How do you think Jesus would rank these? Do you have any evidence to support your choices?

   h. Can you find evidence in the New Testament that shows Jesus was not happy with hypocrisy? downgrading of human life? failure to identify each person as neighbor? actions harming the outcast and the defenseless?

SIX

Law and Freedom

Love and do what you will.
—St. Augustine

Imagine yourself rummaging through the attic and coming across an old, faded photograph of your grandmother taken when she was a young girl. As you blow the dust off the oval frame and look at the picture, you may realize that things have really changed since the picture was taken.

In terms of morality, the comparatively strict attitudes of the past have given way to the more liberal attitudes of today. We consider the stuffy parlors and tight corsets of yesteryear to be reflections of a stuffy and uptight moral prudishness which we have obviously rejected.

Unfortunately, the Catholic church appears to many to be as old-fashioned as grandmother's picture. In fact, many young people are turned off by the church precisely because they are unable to reconcile Christian moral standards with today's free, easygoing, more secular moral standards.

Christian morality upholds challenging ideals. But this does not mean that the law of Christ restricts our true freedom. This chapter will examine how the law of Christ frees us to love God and others in the deepest possible way. But first we must ask ourselves, What is freedom?

The unabridged Webster's offers 19 definitions of *freedom,* one of the most vital concepts known to us, an ideal people have been willing to die for. Here is a partial list of definitions:

a. self-determination
b. exemption or liberation from slavery, imprisonment or restraint, or from the undue, arbitrary or despotic power and control by another

    c. generosity (for example, "freedom and nobility of her soul")

    d. unrestricted use

    e. right or privilege

For our purposes we'll divide freedom into two types: *internal freedom* and *external freedom.* Internal freedom is the freedom to be all we can possibly be. External freedom is freedom of action, the freedom to do all we can possible do.

DEFINING FREEDOM

1. Before discussing internal freedom, complete this open-ended sentence:

   I would feel perfectly free if . . .

   Share and discuss responses.

2. Write your definition of *freedom* here: _____

   _____

   Which definition from the list given above most closely matches your definition?

   _____

3. Look up the word *license.* (Find a definition which is negative in tone, especially when compared to freedom.)

   Write the definition here: _____

   _____

   Discuss: How is license a threat to true freedom?

INTERNAL FREEDOM

Internal freedom, the freedom to be all we can possibly be, is a state of *fulfilled being* rather than a way of acting.

Internal freedom means freedom from such things as isolation, suffering and death, in short, from all that prevents us from being fully alive. Because all of us must die, none of us can attain total internal freedom while on earth. However, we can attain various degrees of internal freedom. And our faith in Jesus Christ gives us the hope of perfect internal freedom after death.

An example of a kind of internal freedom is found in the experience of two people who fall deeply in love. Their love frees them to experience a certain degree of happiness.

But the freedom of this love, for all its power and wonder, is not total and final. A bride, for example, cannot promise her spouse freedom from all suffering; much less can she promise him freedom from death. In short, her love does not have the power to make him *all* he can possibly be.

Nevertheless, the freeing effect of human love is real. Love helps us become what we are meant to be. The daily actions, for example, of a married couple toward each other help them achieve internal freedom—or limit their internal freedom. If a spouse chooses to be unfaithful, that freedom of action becomes the means of limiting what the marriage is meant to be. Our external acts support or limit our freedom to become what we are meant to be in love relationships.

Human love, as known on earth, will end in death; God's love ends in superabundant life. We celebrate Easter to remind ourselves that Jesus offers us participation in his own total victory over death. Our faith in Jesus Christ is grounded there, not in his high moral values or great wisdom. The alleluias sung on Easter morning are in response to Jesus' promise:

> "If anyone believes in me, even though he dies he
> will live,
> and whoever lives and believes in me
> will never die" (Jn 11:26).

He will fulfill his promise because of the gift of the Holy Spirit. St. Paul puts it this way:

> If the Spirit of him who raised Jesus from the dead is
> living in you, then he who raised Jesus from the dead
> will give life to your own mortal bodies through his
> Spirit living in you (Rom 8:11).

We can gain total internal freedom only in heaven. And we

will achieve total internal freedom by means of our attitudes and external actions. Here is where Christian morality plays a vital role. Our moral actions help us achieve the internal freedom of perfect fulfillment in God. Conversely, our immoral actions help prevent us from achieving this ultimate freedom. As with all people in a love relationship, Christians are free to do what they must do in order to be faithful to love. Freedom without this fidelity to love is not freedom but license.

The Adam and Eve story drives home this last point. In freely choosing to disobey God, our first parents chose to undermine their own internal freedom. We can see here the paradoxical truth that moral obligations are in the last analysis obligations to our own freedom. For example, once a husband freely chooses to love his wife, he takes on an obligation to be bound by that love.

It is our freely-made choice not to be true to our love relationships that limits internal freedom. When we choose self over others we truly become prisoners locked in our own selfishness and, hence, less free.

INTERNAL FREEDOM

1. *Read* the story of St. John the Baptist, especially his imprisonment and beheading by Herod (Mt 14:1-12). In what sense was Herod the prisoner and John the one who was free?

2. *Compare* Shakespeare's Romeo in the play *Romeo and Juliet* to the character of Scrooge in Dickens' *A Christmas Carol.* Romeo was hopelessly in love with Juliet. Scrooge, on the other hand, was in love with no one. Scrooge was his own man, yet was he not more imprisoned within himself than Romeo? Does a love relationship take us out of ourselves and give us a taste of internal freedom? Do we need commitment to another to be free? Does love have its own inner laws that bind and yet set us free?

3. *Discuss* the paradoxical statement that in all love relationships we are free to do what we must do in order to be faithful to love.

EXTERNAL FREEDOM

Usually when people speak of freedom they are referring to external freedom—the freedom to do all that we can possibly do. It is the freedom to do what we want when we want.

External freedom is a means of achieving or rejecting internal freedom. If we choose loving union with others, we will experience internal freedom. If we choose to be unfaithful to love, we reject the happiness and fulfillment that it brings.

Friendship, for example, is a love relationship which frees us to be ourselves. We don't need to play games or wear masks with a friend. By the same token, when we deliberately hurt our friends we become less than we should be. Hurt breeds anger and resentment; it eats away at our insides. It doesn't free us at all; it enslaves and embitters us.

What is true of human love is also true of the love that unites us to God. Jesus came to give us the eternal and perfect freedom of sharing in his relationship with the Father by means of the the Spirit of love who sets us free. *Christian moral life is the daily decision to be faithful to this love relationship with God.* By freely choosing to be faithful to the Lord, we experience the internal freedom which union with him brings. In choosing to be unfaithful to him, we experience loss of the peace and strength which are the fruits of being united to him.

There is, then, a paradox to human freedom. The paradox is that we are free to do what love requires of us. In choosing not to respond to love's demands we freely choose not to be free. Thus, we bear within us not only the seeds of our fulfillment in love but the seeds of our destruction as well. This is the meaning of sin—that we freely choose to weaken or destroy our life-giving relationship with God.

CHOOSING FREEDOM

Decide how you would act in the following four situations. Then discuss each of the situations in terms of the relationship between an exercise of external freedom and the experience of internal freedom.

1. Your parents go away for the weekend trusting that you won't have any friends over for a party. What would you do?

   _____

   _____

2. You have promised to go to the prom with someone in your class. A week before the prom another classmate whom you like a lot asks you to go. What would you do?

   _____

   _____

3. The night before an important exam your friends ask you to go to a concert that you want to see very much. What would you do?

   _____

   _____

4. At your job you discover that it is very easy to take money from the petty cash drawer without any danger of being caught. What would you do?

   _____

   _____

THREATS TO FREEDOM

Once we realize the importance of freedom in our lives, we can see why any threat to our freedom is an attack on human dignity, on our vocation to live as God's children.

External Threats to Freedom

External threats to freedom are forces in society which directly or indirectly endanger our quest for internal freedom. These include *oppression, injustice* and *prejudice.*

Events such at the American and French revolutions and movements like the lettuce and grape boycotts, women's liberation, pro-life rallies and protests against nuclear weapons, are examples of the constant need to struggle against the forces of oppression. People, too, like Martin Luther King and Mother Teresa of Calcutta challenge us to overcome forces in society that limit our freedom and the freedom of others. Certainly, Christians must be united with those men and women of good will who work for a free society. The Fathers of the Second Vatican Council wrote:

> Whatever insults human dignity, such as subhuman living conditions, arbitrary imprisonment . . . disgraceful working conditions, where men are treated as mere tools for profit . . . all these things and others of their like are infamies indeed. . . . Moreover, they are a supreme dishonor to the Creator (*Constitution on the Church in the Modern World,* No. 27).

Jesus calls us as a people to work for God's kingdom. We are bound by the love of Christ to work toward bettering society in preparation for the Lord's second coming. We never go to heaven alone. Our call from God comes in and through the society in which we live. We are committed to work for social justice so that all people may find the means to become all they can possibly be. Scripture reveals that social justice is a burning commitment on behalf of the poor, on behalf of those who are victimized by poverty, prejudice and other social ills. Thus, social justice demands that we reach out and secure the God-given rights of those whose freedom is being abused.

Pope John Paul II wrote some wise words on the true meaning of freedom in his first encyclical letter:

> Nowadays it is sometimes held, though wrongly, that freedom is an end in itself, that each human being is free when he makes use of freedom as he wishes, and that this must be our aim in the lives of individuals and societies. In reality, freedom is a great gift only when we know how to use it consciously for everything that is our true good. Christ teaches us that *the best use of freedom is charity, which takes concrete form in self-giving and in service (Redeemer of Man,* No. 21, emphasis added).

EXERCISES

A. *Mini-research.* Get a month's supply of a weekly news magazine and a week's supply of newspapers. Bring to class stories which document:
   1. external threats to freedom, and
   2. examples of international, national and local agencies which are doing something to protect and advance the freedom of individuals.

B. *Rank order* the following groups. Which category needs utmost priority in gaining human rights/freedoms today? (*1* represents the top priority, *10* the lowest.)

_____ battered children

_____ the starving in the world

_____ young people in the church

_____ unborn children

_____ workers in communist countries

_____ women

_____ gays

_____ blacks

_____ victims of violent crime

_____ the handicapped

Discuss:

1. On what basis did you make your judgment?
2. Is there anything you can do right now for the people you listed as your first priority? Explain.

Internal Threats to Freedom

Other threats to freedom come from within. They include ignorance, our passions and our habits. There is an element in each of these which limits our freedom; none of us has perfect control of all our thoughts, emotions and life experiences. At the same time there is an element in each which we can control and for which we are responsible. These aspects are the concern of moral theology.

Ignorance. The lack of knowledge can hurt others as well as ourselves. Suppose, for example, that you have a close friend who is sensitive about a particular aspect of her personality. You, however, find this trait amusing and never miss an opportunity to mention it. Months later your friend tells you about her feelings on this matter. You then realize that in ignorance you have been hurting your relationship with your friend.

Ignorance can also damage our relationship with God. Our responsibility in this matter is to make an honest effort to inform our conscience properly. Deliberately to remain in ignorance about what is required of a mature Christian is morally wrong. We have two obligations in regard to ignorance:

1. To keep an open mind and clear up any wrong information we have.

2. To learn continuously about the obligations of the Christian moral life.

Passions. Emotions affect us both spiritually and physically. They move us to act in a certain way. Passions such as joy, love, fear and sorrow are in themselves good, and they form an important dimension in our lives. Their strong influence, however, can restrict our freedom and possibly lead to immorality.

Some actions have no moral significance. Giving way to our emotions in such circumstances is thus without moral significance; for example, wild enthusiasm at a football game is neither moral nor immoral in itself.

Other actions are directly immoral. Giving way to the emotions that move us to do such things increases our involvement in the action. Furthermore, emotions like fear, hate and sorrow can intensify our involvement in destructive acts. The emotions can become overpowering. Under their influence we can temporarily lose our use of free will and so become dehumanized.

Emotions may limit our moral responsibility. For example, a man's temper might get the better of him. He might do something under its influence that he might not otherwise do.

The moral obligation is to check any emotion that might get out of hand. The person with a short temper has to be aware of those situations where the temper might flare up and cause problems.

There is an old adage in Catholic morality which can serve us quite well: Avoid sin and the near occasions of sin. "Near occasions" are those situations or attitudes which are not sinful in themselves, but which we know from past experience are likely to lead us to sin. Indulging the emotions can be a near occasion of sin for many people.

Passions, once again, are in themselves good. They become evil when directed to dehumanizing actions. The sexual passions involved in marriage, for example, are directed toward a good end; namely, the deepening of love and the procreation of children. Likewise, the joy which close friends delight in at celebrations is directed to enriching their friendship. A stoic rejection of the passions is not part of Christian morality.

FOR DISCUSSION

1. Can you think of some rules you would make for junior high students concerning dating and the use of drugs? These rules should be designed to protect them from any harm they might cause themselves or others because of their lack of experience (that is, ignorance) in regard to these two matters. Try to compose a list of five rules and discuss the wisdom behind them.

2. How can our emotions help us to express love and concern for others? What are some of the effects of being unable to express the strong feelings we might have toward others, for example, feelings of attraction or feelings of anger?

3. Acting out our impulses can hurt both ourselves and others. List some examples. Discuss how the use of alcohol and drugs is related to the loss of the control we should have over our emotions.

4. What would you say to a person who has a short temper? Can you think of some good tips for controlling it?

Habits. One of the funny sights we all delight in is watching a baby learning to feed himself or herself. It is a major victory for the child to find its own mouth! But in no time at all self-feeding becomes a habit for the child.

Habits are second nature to us. They help us do things spontaneously, effortlessly and without thinking. Habits are invaluable. Imagine how it would be if every time you ate you had to begin all over again to learn how to find your mouth!

Habits have significance in our moral life, too. As with the passions, some habits—like the complex skills involved in driving a car—have no particular moral significance. Other habits are what we call virtues; they are good habits. The habits of going out of our way to help others or being courteous are virtues. A virtuous person is one who spontaneously does what is good; he or she has developed good habits. Virtuous living has become a way of life.

Vices are bad habits. They develop from choices which at first called for a deliberate act of the will. For example, the first time a person steals something, he or she might have strong guilt feelings. But if the person keeps stealing, it becomes effortless. By repeating acts of stealing, he or she has become a thief. By lying long enough, a person takes on the identity of a liar. By cheating over a period of time, a person becomes a cheater.

To the extent that a person has been taken over by a particular habit, there is a decreased amount of blameworthiness for what the person is doing. But, by the same token, the individual is bound to avoid doing what is likely to become a bad habit. And, if a person does have a bad habit, he or she has a serious obligation to try to overcome it and replace it with virtuous living.

RATIONALIZATIONS AND VALID EXCUSES

Rationalization means making incorrect but self-satisfying excuses for our behavior—usually wrong behavior. It seems to be part of human nature to take the easy way out, to blame our shortcomings on something or someone else.

Here is a list of comments. Some appear to be valid excuses; others are mere rationalizations. Check those that are probably rationalizations.

_____ 1. "I failed the test because the room was too hot."

_____ 2. "I couldn't study for the test because my boyfriend called me for the first time in two weeks."

_____ 3. "I didn't give to the mission collection because I needed the money for the bus ride home."

_____ 4. "I missed the putt because someone yelled 'fore' during my backswing."

_____ 5. "It would have been stupid not to cheat. The teacher wasn't looking and everybody else was doing it anyhow."

_____ 6. "I punched him out because he called my mother a name."

_____ 7. "I got drunk because I didn't know my limit."

_____ 8. "I didn't know what the speed limit was."

Discuss:
1. What other facts would you like to know in order to judge the items above?
2. Do people too easily excuse themselves and try to justify their wrong behavior? Explain.
3. Good habits are hard to form but easy to break, and bad habits are easy to form but hard to break. Do you think this statement is true?

Virtues: Here is a list of virtues. Which do you admire most in other people? Mark *O* for those you admire in others; mark *S* for those you'd like to work on for yourself.

____ generosity   ____ patience   ____ discipline

____ willingness   ____ persistence   ____ humility
     to work hard
               ____ ability to   ____ honesty
____ ability to   laugh at
     forgive   oneself   ____ purity

WHAT IS LAW?

Freedom is related to law in the way a lake is related to the shore that contains it. Just as the shore gives the lake shape and holds it in its boundaries, so law gives shape to our freedom and marks off its boundaries. Law is a binding rule of conduct that serves to give shape and direction to our freedom.

Law helps our consciences discover the moral obligations we owe to God our Father, to ourselves, and to other persons. It is an objective norm which serves as a guide to doing the right thing. It points to the real world and guides the conscience in fulfilling many duties in regard to God and our fellow creatures.

Our discussion will treat law under four traditional categories: natural, civil, divine and church law.

Natural Law

Nature is bound by certain laws: Water freezes at a certain temperature. Each species of spider spins a web of a particular design. The planets revolve around the sun in precise orbits. The natural sciences attempt to understand these *laws of nature* and how they can serve our needs.

Humans are part of the natural order also, and are bound by what philosophers, theologians and social scientists call *natural law,* that is, standards of human behavior that are discoverable in nature by all people.

An example of a standard found in natural law is "do good and avoid evil." One culture may define what is good differently from another, but both will agree that its members are bound to do what is perceived as good.

Theology is also interested in the natural law. Our faith teaches us that God has established a natural law which manifests itself in our inborn tendency to act in accordance with God's plan to share in his divine life. Being created in God's image and likeness gives us a natural inclination to search out and to do his will.

In its most fundamental manifestation, the natural law prompts us to promote and protect everything that assures our happiness and to avoid everything that endangers it. Natural law manifests itself in our tendency to protect and foster the quality of human life and to be opposed to everything that might threaten it.

Natural law manifests itself in the general human desire to preserve life. Though different societies permit the taking of life in such situations as capital punishment, abortion, and infanticide, human reason tells us that life must be respected and preserved.

Natural law, then, refers to the laws that are contained in the nature of life itself and, through reason, are knowable to all people.

The story of Adam and Eve shows us what happens when human will defies God's plan. The effects of this original sin on our first parents and on subsequent generations tell a dark story of defying the plan for happiness God has written into our very hearts. When we go against the nature of things, we get hurt and we hurt others, too.

Civil Law

The natural law is a general orientation toward that which protects and promotes the quality of human life and, hence, toward our own happiness and the happiness of others. As such, it must be interpreted by each society and applied to specific situations. This social interpretation and application of the natural law is called *civil law.*

Christians are bound to obey all valid civil laws. We see this obligation in Jesus' own command "to give to Caesar the things that are Caesar's." We see it, too, in St. Paul's words: "Let everyone obey the authorities that are over him, for there is no authority except from God, and all authority that exists is established by God" (Rom 13:1, *New American Bible*).

The moral obligation to obey civil authority corresponds to the seriousness of the law in terms of its effect on our well-being and the well-being of others. For example, the law that requires bicycles to have license plates has little moral significance compared to the laws that prohibit the selling of dangerous drugs, or the laws that forbid shooting guns on public streets.

EXERCISE

Listed below are some examples of civil laws. In small groups, do the following:

1. Note the specific interpretation and application of these laws in your own community.
2. Discuss how these laws serve to promote and protect the quality of human life.

- curfew laws
- sanitation laws
- laws prohibiting the sale of alcoholic beverages to minors
- equal housing laws
- minimum-wage laws
- social security laws
- traffic laws

Divine Law

As Christians, we believe that divine revelation is needed to clarify and perfect our knowledge of how God wants us to live. *Divine law* clarifies the demands of the natural law, a law sometimes obscured by our ignorance, passions and habits. These internal threats to freedom can sometimes so blind us that we end up hurting ourselves and others without a full awareness of the immoral behavior we are engaged in.

Civil law, too, is no guarantee that we can overcome the internal threats to freedom. In fact, some civil laws can block our external freedom and prevent us from knowing and following God's will. The Nazi extermination of over six million Jews, the toleration of slavery for centuries, and society allowing abortion on demand are just a few examples of how the members of a society can be permitted by civil laws to act in ways opposed to God's will.

The divine law is revealed in the Ten Commandments and in the person, life and message of Jesus. In short, Jesus commands us to love him and others as he has loved us. The Holy Spirit enables us to follow the divine law, "to imitate God, as children of his that he loves, and follow Christ by loving as he loved you" (Eph 5:1-2).

Church Law

Just as the civil law interprets the natural law, so church law interprets and applies divine law. Church law applies the divine law to the circumstances of Christian life. For example, God's law to keep holy the Lord's day is made specific in the law that we must attend Sunday Mass.

Church laws can change as the Christian community adapts to new circumstances. Our moral obligation to observe church laws relates to the seriousness of the law as it affects our relationship to God and others. Like civil law, church law throws light on the social dimension of our moral life and on our need to respond to God and others in the concrete details of daily life.

In recent years the church has relaxed some of its laws to give Catholics more responsibility in their own moral life. Your grandparents and perhaps your parents remember the old obligation to fast every day during Lent. The law was good in that it made concrete the obligation of every Christian to deny self in imitation of the Lord. Unfortunately, some people responded to the law of fasting legalistically and missed the spirit of the law which was to walk in the footsteps of the Lord during the Lenten season.

The laws of fasting were changed to challenge Catholics to

take more initiative in their own spiritual growth. This freedom has helped many to respond in a more adult way. Other Catholics, though, chose not to do anything special by way of self-denial after the law was eased. Freedom is found not in throwing off laws but in making them part of our own personal response and commitment to Jesus Christ.

DISCUSSION

1. Your parents tell you that they don't want you to drink when you go out on a date. Discuss your obligation to obey them with respect to:

   a. the natural law

   b. civil law

   c. divine law

2. The Catholic community keeps holy the Lord's day by celebrating the Eucharist. Some Catholics go to Mass only to fulfill an obligation. Others go primarily to express their desire to remain faithful to Christ as part of a worshiping community.

   a. Which of the two attitudes do you think is characteristic of most Catholics? of your classmates? of yourself?

   b. Is the church law to attend Mass necessary? Why or why not?

3. Obtain a copy of your school's student handbook.

   a. List and discuss various regulations which clearly attempt to protect the rights of students and the quality of education in your school.

   b. Which regulations should be revised or dropped? Why?

   c. Could you and your classmates do without school rules? Why or why not?

4. What do you suppose St. Augustine meant when he said "Love and do what you will"? Does love free us from the observance of laws? Or does love help us to see the wisdom behind laws and prompt us to fulfill their requirements? Explain. What do you think Jesus meant when he said he came to fulfill the law?

SUMMARY

1. Christians are called to be free. Internal freedom is the freedom to be all we can possibly be; external freedom is the freedom to do all we can possibly do.

2. Freedom without commitment and fidelity to love is not true freedom, but license.

3. Any threat to human freedom is an attack on human dignity. Thus, external threats to freedom like oppression, injustice and prejudice make it more difficult for us to live our vocation as God's children.

4. Internal threats to human freedom include ignorance (the lack of knowledge or wrong information), the passions (emotions) and habits (learned behaviors which we do with little conscious thought). We have a moral obligation to overcome ignorance concerning right and wrong, to control our emotions, and to work to overcome bad habits (vices) and replace them with good habits (virtues).

5. Law is a binding rule of conduct that guides us in doing the right thing.

   a. The natural law, discoverable in creation, calls us to act in accordance with God's plan to share in his divine life.

   b. Civil law is the particular application of the natural law for a given society.

   c. Divine law, found in the Old and New Testaments, clarifies the demands of natural law.

   d. Church law applies divine law to the concrete circumstances of Christian life.

APPLICATION

Draft Registration: Think about the following situation:

> You have an 18-year-old friend who is pondering whether he should register for the draft as the law requires. He loves his country but suspects that preparing for war and spending billions of dollars on bigger and more destructive weapons violates the call to Jesus to witness to peace. Your friend thinks he might be involved in a terrible moral wrong by cooperating with the government law to register for the draft. If he doesn't register, he is subject to a $10,000 fine and a prison term. Furthermore, his parents probably won't understand his position, and he may jeopardize future employment opportunities.

Your friend has asked your advice. What would you say to him?

Discuss: After you've thought about the advice you would give, discuss the following questions as a class:

1. Is this a crystal-clear case of a divine law in conflict with the civil law? Why or why not?

2. Does a government have the right to protect its people?

3. Research the just-war theory. Does the theory apply to the use of nuclear weapons? What is the church's position on the nuclear arms race?

4. In what kind of war must a Catholic not participate?

5. What do you think Jesus meant when he said "Blessed are the peacemakers"?

6. Is it Christian to defend one's country? Is it Christian to be a pacifist?

SEVEN

What's This Thing Called Sin?

It is not easy to die even for a good man—though of course for someone really worthy, a man might be prepared to die—but what proves that God loves us is that Christ died for us while we were still sinners.

—St. Paul

A discussion of Christian morality will eventually lead to a consideration of sin. If we admit that Jesus Christ came to save sinners, then it is important for us to discuss the nature of sin and its relationship to Christian living.

WHY ALL THIS TALK ABOUT SIN?

A major problem with the topic of sin is trying to talk meaningfully about it. One of the major charges leveled against Christians is that we tend to overemphasize sin. Some people maintain that too much talk about sin results in a "fire-and-brimstone" approach to religion where fear of hell and eternal damnation is given primary emphasis. Consequently, these people see Christianity as a joyless religion, too negative in its approach to the problems of the world.

RECALL

Can you remember the last time a "fire-and-brimstone" sermon was preached to you? What was your reaction to it?

119

The above criticism of Christianity is not fair. Christianity is a joyful religion precisely because it claims that sin and its consequences can be overcome. But Christianity is also fundamentally realistic because it recognizes our human condition. It tries to articulate what has been, what should be and what can be done about it.

THE CONCEPT OF SIN

Many people today prefer not to talk about sin, but the concept has validity nonetheless. We Christians believe that humanity has progressed over the centuries. Today we benefit from the advances of science which have brought us a higher standard of living than our ancestors had. We work fewer hours; we live longer lives; we enjoy many freedoms not dreamed of even a hundred years ago.

Humans are capable of great progress and much good; by the same token, we have certain destructive tendencies. We are both builders and destroyers; we are living paradoxes. Evidences of evil and sin in the world are present all around us. Note the following examples:

War. World War I was labeled the "war that would end all wars." Yet 20 short years after the completion of that war, the nations of the world were once again using their knowledge for destructive purposes. More recently, the Vietnam War resulted in internal strife in our own country, loss of respect abroad and a widespread economic recession. And now, as one theologian put it, "We have created the end of the world and stored it in our silos." The insanity of the arms race dwarfs most moral problems facing us today.

Prejudice. Job and housing discrimination based on religion, race, or sex is still with us. Discrimination against the poor, the weak and defenseless, and people who are different is documented in our daily newspapers. Prejudice resulted in Hitler's attempt to eradicate the Jewish people during the Second World War. Today, a similar holocaust is directed against innocent unborn babies who are aborted "to solve a problem." We live in a throwaway society which judges people by what they can do; if they are not useful, they can be eliminated.

Corruption. Young people are cynical about the greed, corruption and lying found in government. Price-fixing in big business, income-tax cheating, shoplifting and lack of an "honest day's work for an honest day's pay" are phenomena of today's society. Exploitation of the poor in the marketplace is a depressing daily reality in our world.

Much evil in the world results from inhumanity, from people's failure to live constructively. To the degree that we knowingly and freely refuse to live as God's children called to love others, we sin. Of course, there is much evil in the world for which humanity does not seem directly responsible; cosmic calamities such as tornados, earthquakes, and other natural forces are part of the great mystery of evil.

EXERCISES

A. *Personal Sin*: Consider the following:

> John has just returned from a weekend spiritual renewal with the youth group of his parish. It was a most worthwhile experience for him. He made a resolution on the retreat to break his habit of cheating. He does OK for a while but soon finds himself copying a friend's homework. Despite his firm resolve, John has found himself cheating again.

Many of us, no doubt, have found ourselves in similar situations. We try to break a bad habit only to find ourselves falling back into it again. This tells us something about the nature of sin. Even a Christian giant like St. Paul recognized the problem: "I cannot understand my own behavior. I fail to carry out the things I want to do, and I find myself doing the very things I hate" (Rom 7:15). We are sinners; we are weak in resisting the wrong thing.

Reflection: Think of some resolution you have made and broken. What should we do in the face of this all-too-human situation? Give up? Try again? Ask our Lord for help? What do you do?

B. *Prejudice*: Prejudice is one of the great moral evils today. It can result in stereotyping, that is, oversimplifying our description of people or things. Stereotyping can be favorable, but rarely is; it usually is quite uncomplimentary and even degrading of others.

Can you recognize a stereotype when you see one? Which of the following seem to be stereotypes, the result of prejudiced thinking?

1. Women are incapable of performing as well as men in careers like law, government and medicine.
2. The government should make an effort to look into welfare fraud because sometimes welfare recipients cheat.
3. Homosexuals should not be allowed to teach because they are noted child molesters.
4. Our judicial system seems to work better for people who are white and have a certain income.
5. Women who are raped deserve it because they usually wear provocative clothing.
6. Grades are easier to come by in colleges today than they were 20 years ago.
7. Alcoholics have no respect for life.

Discuss:

1. What harm is done by stereotyping?
2. What would Jesus say about judging others falsely?
3. What are some stereotypes people your age have? What about people of your parents' generation?
4. What can be done about stereotyping?

WHAT IS SIN?

The Bible is a good place to turn to get some insight into sin. The Old Testament, for example, tells the story of a people who struggled to live a life of obedience to their loving God. It records their shortcomings and gives some great psychological insights into the nature of sin.

What emerges from reading the Old Testament is that God is very interested in his people. He called them to life and gave them a land to live on. In return he asked that his people adore him and love one another in gratitude for the love he showered on them. The Old Testament describes sin as a break or lessening of this living, personal relationship with a loving Father.

The scripture reveals that pride is often at the root of our stiff-necked refusal to love God or others. In the story of Adam and Eve we see that pride and stubbornness led to our first parents' disobedience of God's command. Pride cut off the living relationship between God and them, and led ultimately to death.

Scripture presents this living relationship in terms of a covenant, an agreement of love between God and his people to be faithful to one another. God was always loyal to the Chosen People even though they were not always faithful. In the Old Testament, terms like "stiff-necked," "hardhearted people," "missing the mark" and "stubborn" mark the people's failure to live up to the covenant.

> "But this people
> has a rebellious, unruly heart;
> they have rebelled—being good at this!" (Jer 5:23).

The New Testament also talks about sin in terms of relationship. Jesus affirmed that the greatest commandments had to do with a loving relationship: first, loving God above all things; and second, loving your neighbor as yourself. The first commandment drives home the importance of loving and worshiping God—this is our primary duty. Many of our sins of failure to love flow from idolatry of other things—making things or self more worthy of worship than God. The second tells us how to act toward others, our brothers and sisters in Jesus.

FALSE GODS

Discuss how the following may be worshiped, that is, made into gods:

- sex
- alcohol and drugs
- what others think of us

- money
- another person
- power

The Social Dimension of Sin

The Old Testament stressed that the breaking of the covenant with God was often a *community* failure. Because one person was not loving, the whole community in its relationship to one another and to God suffered. The prophet Amos was especially sensitive to the social dimension of sin when he railed against the social injustices done to the poor and the downtrodden.

Jesus also saw sin as a failure to love others. He identified the love of God with the love of neighbor; failing to love the "least of these" was a failure to love God. He said that our judgment in the afterlife would be based on how we responded to all members of the community, especially the least fortunate.

St. Paul expresses a similar notion in his famous Body of Christ imagery. In the Spirit of Jesus and his Father we are one; through the blood of Christ we are related to one another. Because we are children of God, there must be a social concern for all. Thus the argument used by some to justify abortion is false; namely, that a woman has a right to her own body. Rather, the new life in her body belongs to the whole community, the human family, not just to the individual mother. Likewise, when a child dies of starvation, one of our brothers and sisters has died. Our failure to be concerned with the poor—a vivid example of a lack of love—has tremendous social consequences.

FOR DISCUSSION

In what way might each of the following be called a "community sin"?

- endangering your life through reckless skiing
- spreading rumors about another person
- ignoring a person who is in need of help
- failing to exercise the right to vote
- failing to be concerned about the nuclear arms race

Sin and Attitudes

Our sinful actions don't just happen. They flow from our inner attitudes. When questioned by the Pharisees and scribes about why he and his disciples did not wash their hands before eating a meal, Jesus answered that the external act flows from the inner attitude:

> "Listen, and understand. What goes into the mouth does not make a man unclean; it is what comes out of the mouth that makes him unclean. . . . For from the heart come evil intentions: murder, adultery, fornication, theft, perjury, slander. These are the things that make a man unclean. But to eat with unwashed hands does not make a man unclean" (Mt 15:10-11, 19-20).

Sin is rooted primarily in the heart. Our attitudes lead to our actions or failures to act when we clearly should. The parable of the Good Samaritan illustrates this well. The priest and Levite sinned because they failed to love the injured victim. Their basic attitude was not to get involved with the foreigner, so they decided not to act. But Jesus taught that our neighbor includes the foreigner, even the enemy, and that love of neighbor exists by positively acting on his or her behalf. Those who fail to act do so because of a fundamental attitude of indifference, of not caring. The sin illustrated in this famous parable is a sin of omission.

Basic attitudes can lead to sins of commission too. Many of these sins are catalogued in the Ten Commandments: idolatry, blasphemy, disrespect, disobedience, killing, theft, lying, cheating and the like. Disobedience toward authority, for example, often flows from a person's basic attitude of pride, of believing that "no one can tell me what to do." Likewise, sins of sexuality often flow from selfish attitudes of pleasure-seeking and self-indulgence. In both cases, the acts flow from attitudes.

EXERCISES

A. *Discuss*: How do *attitudes* of hostility lead to acts of:
- killing
- jealousy
- discrimination
- backbiting

Discuss: How do *attitudes* of concern lead to acts of:
- sharing
- caring
- getting involved

B. Here are three definitions of sin. Which one makes the most sense to you?
- Sin is a rejection of God's love, a refusal to accept his love and share it with others.
- Sin is basically a personal offense against God, a turning away from him.
- Sin is any deliberate unfaithfulness to God's will.

As a class come up with several examples which would clearly fit each of these definitions.

Read and reflect: Carefully read the parable of the Good Samaritan, Luke 10:25-37. Rewrite this parable to fit today's world.

WHEN AM I GUILTY OF SIN?

Before answering the question posed by this section we should distinguish between two concepts: being *responsible* for particular actions, and being *blameworthy* for them.

I am responsible, meaning "answerable," for my actions and attitudes. For example:

a. Did I run the red light? Yes.

b. Did I make a mistake on my income tax? Yes.

c. Did I hit you with a golf ball? Yes.

The above were *my* actions. I am answerable for them. I have to admit that I did them.

On the other hand, I may or may not be blameworthy. I am blameworthy only if I have moral guilt for my actions. For example:

a. Yes, I ran the red light, but I could see that no one was coming, and I was taking a critically injured child to the hospital. I am responsible for my action, but not blameworthy.

b. Yes, I made a mistake on my income tax, an accidental error in addition when tallying my deductions. I am responsible for my action, but since I did not intend it, there is no moral guilt.

c. Yes, I hit you with a golf ball. I intended to do so. I didn't particularly like the fact that you were beating me by 15 strokes, so I deliberately aimed one of my shots right at you. I am both responsible *and* blameworthy.

Besides the concepts of responsibility and blameworthiness, we need to deal with the distinction between *mortal* and *venial* sin. Some sins, some failures to love, are more serious than others. Mortal sin is a rejection of God's love—it kills God's life and love within us. To commit mortal sin, the action or attitude must be a serious rejection of God's love. In addition, the person must know that it is serious and decide to do it anyway.

Venial sin weakens but does not kill our love relationship

with God and neighbor. It makes us less able to nurture God's loving presence within us. Venial sin involves offenses that are not serious, or that the person does not fully recognize as serious, or that the person does not wholeheartedly want to do.

With these distinctions in mind, let us answer the question, When am I guilty of sin?

1. *Is it wrong?* Do I have an attitude or have I performed an action which does indeed destroy the relationship between God and me or between me and my neighbor? Clearly a nasty word spoken to a classmate does not help our relationship; it usually harms it. But a nasty word ordinarily is not so serious as to destroy totally my relationship to my classmate, or my relationship to God.

On the other hand, my deliberately fostered attitude of hostility toward members of another race is serious; it destroys relationship. It constitutes *mortal* sin because it kills the relationship.

2. *Do I know it is wrong?* Certainly I am not blameworthy for something I do not know is wrong (although I may be responsible). For example, a person may claim that he or she did not realize that drinking to the point of losing self-control is a serious matter. But giving up our ability to think, choose and judge is indeed serious because it destroys a fundamental part of what it means to be human. Once a person realizes this, he or she has a serious obligation to avoid drunkenness in the future.

While we are not blameworthy for actions committed due to ignorance which was not our fault, we cannot just "hide our heads in the sand" either. We have an obligation to remain open to new knowledge as we grow in deeper and fuller relationship with God and others.

3. *Do I freely engage in the evil?* Not only must my action (or non-action) be wrong in itself, not only must I know it is wrong, but I must also choose to do it freely and willingly. If I steal something—an act that is wrong and that I know is wrong—but I do so because I am being forced to at gunpoint, then I am not blameworthy for the action because I did not freely choose to do it.

MORTAL SIN

The following have traditionally been considered serious matters which tend to kill the love relationship with God and with others. Therefore, if knowledge and free consent of the will are present, mortal sin is involved. Why is each of the following a *serious* rupture in a love relationship?

- apostasy (knowing the truth of Jesus Christ, but then denying him)
- sexual intercourse before marriage
- refusing to help someone in great need
- hating or seriously injuring the reputation of another
- aggressive war
- murder
- divorce
- adultery

What would you add to this list? What would you consider the greatest harm a person could do to a friend? Why?

JESUS AND SIN

How does Jesus Christ fit into our discussion of sin? He is at the very center! Jesus came as the Father's Word to forgive sin and to announce that his Father loves sinners, even the worst kind. Furthermore, his death and resurrection demolished the worst effect of sin—our own death. Through Jesus we have been saved and are able to share an eternal life in union with him and his Father in the power of the Holy Spirit.

First, Jesus forgave sin. His healing ministry demonstrated that God wills wholeness, that he wishes us to be healed from the wounds of alienation caused by sin. Many of his miracles demonstrate that he has come to conquer the ill effects of sin—sickness, brokenness, fragmentation, alienation. His news of God's unbelievable love for us disturbed many of the pious of his day. For example, when Jesus forgave the sins of the paralytic, the religious leaders severely criticized him. They didn't want to believe that Jesus had such power. They didn't want to believe the good news of God's love.

Second, time and again Jesus proclaimed that God loves the sinner. The parable of the Prodigal Son was directed against those who mumbled about Jesus' association with the tax collectors, the prostitutes and various other sinners of the day. In that parable Jesus taught that God loves everyone, that he extends his forgiveness to the worst of sinners. This is marvelous news even today: God loves and forgives sinners, even people like us.

Third, Jesus' death and resurrection showed that death does not have the last word; life is not absurd. By his resurrection Jesus overcame sin and death. Our response should be one of great joy and hope in the face of our own weakness, sinfulness and death.

We Christians believe, furthermore, that Jesus left the power to forgive sin with his church. In the sacrament of reconciliation we encounter the healing Jesus, the forgiving Jesus, and the loving Father who welcomes us with his unconditional, unlimited love.

As individual Christians and as a community bound to the Lord, we all have the responsibility to show others the forgiveness of the Lord:

"And forgive us our debts,
as we have forgiven those who are in debt to us"
   (Mt 6:12).

By forgiving others "even 70 times 7" we help them see that the good news is happening even now. We Christians must be examples—the "salt of the earth" and the "light of the world."

Jesus teaches another important lesson: God's forgiveness is always available to us, but it does not reach the hearts of those who harbor enmity toward others:

"If you are bringing your offering to the altar and there remember that your brother has something against you, leave your offering there before the altar, go and be reconciled with your brother first, and then come back and present your offering" (Mt 5:23-24).

FORGIVENESS

A. God's forgiveness given in the person of Jesus leads to healing—a making whole. Likewise, our extension of God's forgiveness to others helps heal the festering wounds caused by hate. Discuss how a healthy dose of forgiveness could help to heal the following situations:

   • the tensions in the Middle East

   • the issues involved in Women's Liberation

   • disputes between management and labor

   • the issues which have divided different Christian denominations

   • a particular problem you might be having with someone

B. One theologian has remarked that Jesus doesn't mean much to some people because they don't admit that they need forgiveness for anything. Unless we admit that we are sinners in need of divine help, Jesus isn't going to make much difference in our lives. Do you agree with this observation? Why or why not?

SUMMARY

1. Although some people don't like talking about sin, Christians recognize the reality of sin and evil and our need for divine help to overcome them.

2. The Old Testament sees sin as the breaking of a covenant with a loving God.

3. The New Testament clarifies the true nature of sin: the failure to love God and to love neighbor as oneself. Thus, all sin has a social dimension; it has an impact on our relationship to God, to others and to ourselves.

4. Sinful acts flow from sinful attitudes. Sinful attitudes lead both to sins of commission and to sins of omission (that is, failures to act when we should).

5. Moral blameworthiness implies personal guilt. Mortal sin kills God's love in us; it is a rejection of his love. Venial sin weakens our love relationships with God and others.

6. Three conditions are necessary for a person to sin mortally: the matter must be *seriously evil,* the person must have *full knowledge* that it is an evil, and the person must *freely choose* it.

7. Jesus came to destroy sin and its ultimate effect—death. He is our Savior. The sacrament of reconciliation extends his forgiving touch to us today. As his disciples, we are to forgive others as well.

RECONCILIATION

You and your classmates may wish to celebrate the sacrament of reconciliation. If so, plan a real *celebration,* a meaningful encounter with the forgiving Lord.

Our Lord invites us to seek his love the way the younger son did in the parable of the Prodigal Son. And, like the father in the parable, the Lord stands ready to embrace us and "throw a party" because we are willing to return to him.

We can all grow in the spiritual life. We all have some area in our life which the Lord can help heal. Catholics have found an *examination of conscience* a helpful means of growing in self-understanding, of uncovering those attitudes and actions which may keep us from being the loving children we are meant to be.

Here is an examination based on the Beatitudes. Judge for yourself how much you need to grow on each of the points examined. You might use this examination as a preparation for the sacrament of reconciliation.

- Prayerfully read the Beatitudes, Matthew 5:3-12, and the parable of the Prodigal Son, Luke 15:11-32

- Check those items which need work or healing.

_____ Am I truly poor in spirit? Am I greedy? Do I envy what others have? Am I satisfied with the gifts God has given me? Am I grateful for them?

_____ Do I use my material goods wisely? Do I share them? Do I show concern for those less fortunate than I am?

_____ Do I empathize with others? Do I seek out those who are hurt and lonely? Or am I selfish? Do I pity myself too much? Do I have too high an opinion of myself?

_____ Do I truly hunger and thirst for holiness? Do I pray? Do I respect God's name? that of Mary, his mother? Do I participate at Mass or only grudgingly go or not go at all?

_____ Do I show mercy? Do I forgive others? Or do I hold grudges? Do I tend to dominate others by always having to be right and the center of attention? Do I have a short temper?

_____ Am I truly single-hearted, putting God above all things? Or do I put other things like material possessions ahead of him? Do I cheat in order to get ahead? Is sexual pleasure and using other people for my own purposes a key fault? Or am I a slave to liquor or some other drug?

_____ Am I a peacemaker? Am I the kind of person others want to be around? Do I brag? Do I cause problems at home by disobedience or through disrespect? Do I cause problems by lying, spreading rumors, damaging the reputation of others?

_____ Am I willing to suffer for my beliefs? Or do I buckle under pressure and go along with the crowd? Am I honest even if it hurts? Do I accept responsibility for my mistakes and confess my faults? Do I admit that I'm not perfect and need God's help to be a better son or daughter to him? Or am I too proud?

EIGHT

Sexual Morality

Be (of love) a little more careful than of everything.
—e.e. cummings

A high school student once remarked that he first started liking girls the moment he discovered they weren't boys. He may have been exaggerating, but it is no exaggeration to say that male-female relationships play an important part in a teenager's life. Beginning around puberty, these relationships often become among the most alluring and exciting of all life's mysteries.

However, discovering members of the opposite sex often brings with it social awkwardness and misunderstanding. There is so much to learn about the physical, emotional and social aspects of our sexuality. In addition, there are important moral questions that must be faced by any young adult who is seriously trying to live the Christian life.

This chapter attempts to provide a Christian orientation to these moral questions by placing human sexuality in the context of the Christian vision of the human person.

ATTITUDE SURVEY

Divide into groups of two or three. Write a short response to each of the following statements. You may express agreement or disagreement but try to explain how you see each issue.

1. Because the gift of human sexuality is so sacred, sexual intercourse should be expressed only in marriage.

2. Some song lyrics are clearly immoral because they advocate sexual irresponsibility.

3. Many movies blatantly use sex to attract audiences; a lot of times, the appeal to sex is simply not a necessary part of the story.

4. Parents and the church are generally too conservative on the issue of sexual morality.

Discuss the opinions of each of the small groups with the rest of the class.

SEXUALITY AND BEING HUMAN

When the topics of sex and religion are brought together, some people tend to think of sex negatively, in terms of what the church teaches is sinful about certain sexual acts. To overcome this narrow and sin-centered attitude about Christian sexual morality, let us look at the church's very positive teaching about the nature of human sexuality.

Much of church teaching is based on the natural law which holds that to be human is to be either female or male. In other words, to be human is to be sexual in our very being. Being male or female affects most (if not all) of our daily actions.

The changing role of women in our contemporary society serves as an interesting example of how sexuality affects our daily lives. Not too many years ago, it was generally accepted that men and women reacted to situations differently. People "knew" that women, being more emotional, usually cry when they are upset; men, who are more logical, are not supposed to cry. Similarly, it was believed, women were "unable" to handle certain jobs; women were, however, "instinctively superior" to men at raising children.

Of course, there are some basic and important psychological differences between men and women which directly affect their thinking, feeling and acting in different situations. Today we are aware, however, that these differences are not solely a result of gender. To a greater or lesser extent they result from the expectations of our parents and others who have influenced our view of how men "ought" to act and women "ought" to act. For example, it seems true that women cry more frequently than men when they are upset. But it is also true that little girls learn that it is acceptable for them to cry, while boys are told that it is not "manly" to cry. Likewise, it is true that in the past women seldom played a dominant role in politics, science or business. But neither were they encouraged to enter these fields; in fact, they were often forbidden to do so.

The changing role of women demonstrates the profound and far-reaching effects sexuality has on self-image, ways of acting and role expectations. Our sexuality is clearly not only a genital reality; rather, it is a fundamental dimension of our humanity affecting our whole life and everything we do. From this we can begin to see a key principle of Christian sexual morality: *What we do as sexual beings should strengthen and confirm rather than weaken or cloud over our essential human dignity.*

ROLES

Characteristics. Consider the following traits. Put a check (✔) in the column of the sex which would tend to exhibit the trait to a greater degree.

	Male	Female
Ability to bear pain	_____	_____
Feeling hurt or upset	_____	_____
Aggressiveness	_____	_____

Showing feelings	_____	_____
Expertise in infant care	_____	_____
Independence	_____	_____
Creativity	_____	_____
Sensitivity to the feelings of others	_____	_____

Discuss how women tend to react in these circumstances as compared to men. Do you feel these traits are due to basic genetic differences between the sexes or to society's expectations?

SEXUALITY AND FAMILY RELATIONSHIPS

Further insight into the significance and dignity of human sexuality is gained by examining the love relationships that unite the members of a family. Consider the relationships charted below:

```
                    Father————Mother
                            |
Son #1————Son #2————Daughter #1————Daughter #2
   |                                        |
Girlfriend                            Boyfriend of
of Son #1                             Daughter #2
```

The masculinity or femininity of the different family members obviously affects the way in which they relate to one another. Certainly being a mother differs from being a father. There is also a basic difference between a father-son and a father-daughter relationship, just as there is a difference between a mother-son and a mother-daughter relationship.

Furthermore, the way in which sexuality is *expressed* also determines the nature of the relationship. For example, Son #1 doesn't feel the same way about his girlfriend as he does about his sisters. Nor does his girlfriend feel the same way about his brother as she does about him (at least Son #1 hopes she doesn't!).

The relationship between the mother and father is unique. They are the only two who have made a commitment unto death to be faithful to each other. Likewise, they are the only two who can morally engage in sexual relations as an expression of this commitment. Placing their sexual activity in the context of a family is critical to understanding the basis of Christian sexual morality.

Their sexual union not only was the source of life for their children, it is also an outward bodily expression of their total gift of themselves to each other. Sexual intercourse implies a revealing and sharing of a person's total self. This self-surrender and giving is the very basis of love, and it is thus that engaging in sexual intercourse is often spoken of as making love. As we have seen before, relationship with another implies responsibility for that relationship; the deeper the relationship, the deeper the responsibility.

Sexual love is mysterious. It comes from the depths of the heart. It implies a deep-felt union that brings with it tremendous potential to develop and strengthen the two involved, or to hurt and dehumanize them. To go all the way in sexual sharing is proper only between two people who have gone all the way in the broader context of a commitment to share the responsibility that goes with such a deep relationship. Sexual intercourse in marriage is consistent with the married couple's whole life together; sexual intercourse outside marriage is unworthy of the name of love in its deepest dimensions.

The incarnation of Jesus Christ, the Son of God, teaches us that humans have great dignity. Human sexuality also has dignity because it is so central to being human. We must constantly strive to see the power and beauty of sexuality if we are to view it in a Christian context, and thus come to understand the basis of Christian sexual morality. This understanding sees sexuality in terms of committed love and family relationships.

Sometimes books dealing with the morality of premarital

sex focus on negative consequences: venereal disease, unwanted pregnancy, broken family relationships, and so forth.
Certainly the young person must be aware that such dangers are
very real. These dangers may well serve as a deterrent to
premarital sex, but they don't contribute to a positive concept of
sexuality. We must base sexual morality not on what is wrong in
immoral sexual acts, but rather on what is good in moral sexual
acts.

TO THINK ABOUT

A. The following excerpt is from *The Velveteen Rabbit* by
   Margery Williams Bianco. The dialogue involves two
   stuffed animals who are discussing what it means to be
   real.

   > "Does it happen all at once, like being wound
   > up," he asked, "or bit by bit?"
   >
   > "It doesn't happen all at once," said the Skin
   > Horse. "You become. It takes a long time. That's
   > why it often doesn't happen to people who break
   > easily, or have sharp edges, or who have to be
   > carefully kept. Generally, by the time you are real,
   > most of your hair has been rubbed off, and your
   > eyes drop out, and you get loose in the joints and
   > very shabby. But these things don't matter at all,
   > because once you are real, you can't be ugly, except
   > to people who don't understand."

   Discuss:

   1. What does the Skin Horse mean by "being real"? Would
      these same ideas apply to the meaning of love?

   2. Ask a happily married couple, perhaps your parents or
      grandparents, if their marital love is similar to the Skin
      Horse's concept of being real.

   3. In your view, what does it mean to be real?

B. What is the difference between having fun and being happy? Apply the distinction between fun and happiness to the
   difference between a hedonistic (*Playboy* or *Playgirl*)
   philosophy of sex and the approach suggested in the
   quotation given above.

All of this idealistic talk about the meaning of sex in marriage might seem removed from the more practical moral problems facing you as an adolescent. Perhaps this is true to a certain degree. But we only truly understand something by seeing it in terms of what it is at its best. For example, the art of cooking is not appreciated by eating only burned food. Likewise, true skill in a game of soccer is not measured by the neighborhood pickup game, but rather by the professionals who have honed their talents to a thing of beauty.

The same holds true in trying to understand sexual morality. We must all face the questions of sexual morality in light of the fullness and beauty of married love. By acknowledging the trials, the depth, the beauty and fulfillment of marital love, we can all come to see that sex is not a toy. To abuse God's gift of sexuality is to abuse a deep expression of love that gives birth to new love and to new human life. In short, all of us—young people and those who are older—must struggle to judge questions of sexual morality with an ever-maturing Christian conscience.

CHURCH TEACHING

Christian marriage is a sacrament because it is a sign of God's love, a concrete and meaningful sign of the love affair God has with his people. Just as God attaches no conditions to his love for us, the husband and wife in a Christian marriage attach no conditions to their love.

Sexual intercourse is a symbol of the love between the husband and wife. It is a real sign which communicates the true relationship between the man and woman: a "no-strings-attached" kind of love. Of its nature it has two purposes: It is a deep sharing of love between the couple, and it has the potential for transmitting human life.

The Lord teaches that sexual intercourse demands the kind of total, unconditional commitment that can only be found in a marriage, in a covenant of love where the couple has publicly proclaimed their unconditional love for each other. Thus the church teaches that sexual intercourse and all acts leading directly to it (for example, becoming sexually aroused through petting) are reserved for those who have made the kind of commitment, marriage, which these serious, holy, joyful actions do in fact represent.

The church's teaching, which is a call to be faithful to the Lord's teaching, is not basically a set of restrictions on unmarried people; rather, church teaching affirms what is truly beautiful, precious and unique about the power to give ourselves *totally* to another. This teaching also underscores that parenthood and the powers that make it possible are gifts from God, a true sharing in the transmission of new life.

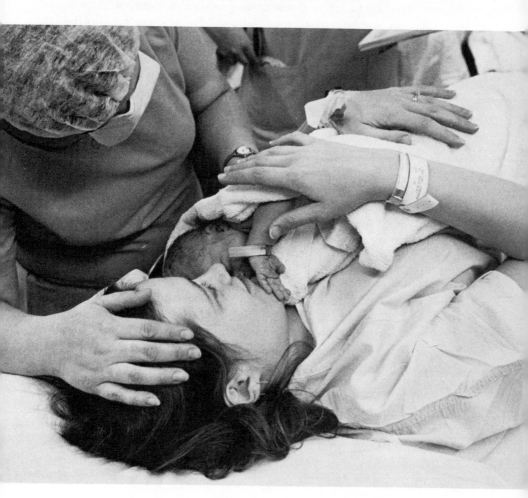

DISCUSSION

1. As a class project, compose a list of attitudes and actions in regard to teen-age sexuality which can help build healthy relationships for a future marriage. Make a similar list of actions and attitudes which might threaten later commitments as a spouse and parent.

2. Why is it important for a young man and woman to be open and honest about their feelings for one another, including the way they express their affection? Why is it difficult to be open about such personal matters?

3. Is it difficult to discuss personal problems and concerns in the area of sexual morality with parents? Why or why not? Are any of the following helpful sources of guidance on issues of sexual morality for you?

   - a counselor
   - a friend
   - a confessor in the sacrament of reconciliation
   - an older brother or sister
   - a trusted teacher
   - a relative
   - a parish priest

THE DIFFICULT STRUGGLE

The young Catholic who tries to live up to the standards of Christian sexual morality is in for a difficult struggle. Sexual issues are rarely neat and clearly defined like problems in a math book. Rather, the sex drive is strong, mysterious and sometimes seems to have a mind of its own. And it can be strongest during the years of adolescent growth and development.

There are also social reasons why a young person's search for high sexual ideals is difficult. One difficulty is the matter of delayed marriage. In almost all past cultures, and still in some today, people married shortly after the onset of puberty. Not so in our culture. Due to factors such as educational requirements and the complexities of the modern economic world, marriage today is often delayed until the mid-20s or even later.

The Catholic community holds that genital sexual expression should be reserved for marriage. Self-control, sacrifice and purity in thought, word and deed are the virtues which young people (in fact, all Christians) are called to live in their struggle to be faithful to Jesus' ideal. But this causes problems, especially between young people who feel strongly about each other, and who have been dating for some time, or may be engaged, yet know they have several years before getting married.

Another social problem is today's widespread sensuality and permissiveness. These put pressure on young people to conform to what is often simply immoral behavior.

Surely, today, we smile at the old song lyrics:

A rooty toot toot,
a rooty toot toot,
we're the boys from the Institute.
We don't smoke,
and we don't chew,
and we don't go with girls who do.

Such sentiments went out with the horse and buggy. In many ways it is a blessing that we have emerged from the prudish ways of yesteryear. But the problem is that the pendulum has swung so far in the opposite direction. For a high school boy to admit that he doesn't have "experience" is like admitting he sleeps with a teddy bear or uses a Mickey Mouse toothbrush. And 15-year-old girls, worried because they are still virgins, occasionally share in letters to Ann Landers their fears that they are "abnormal."

Sexual attitudes have changed since your parents' day, and have changed very dramatically since the days of your grandparents. What was formerly done in secret is now done openly, and the mass media and public opinion condone such action by their lack of criticism, or even promote the "new morality" by presenting it as up-to-date and glamorous. Christians appear to be swimming against the tide of public opinion. But we Christians are called to be different. Our vocation is to witness to the preciousness of human sexuality, its beauty, its rootedness in a relationship of total commitment.

Our Lord asks much of us. But we have one thing on our side: Christian sexual morality is both positive and filled with common sense. The discipline that is required in adolescence to uphold Christian ideals is excellent preparation for the discipline that later is required to maintain a healthy, happy and lasting marriage. When two people care about each other, their concerns about the future make it easier to set and maintain standards for the present.

A second point worth noting is that the source of our strength and direction in maintaining Christian values comes from our personal commitment to and relationship with Jesus Christ. Personal prayer and a sincere desire to do God's will as revealed by Jesus is essential in every aspect of life, including our sexual attitudes and behavior.

SEXUAL VALUES

A. Examine your own values. Use these symbols to mark the following statements:

   \+   agree

   –   disagree

   ?   unsure

   _____ 1. Sexual intercourse should reflect total giving, commitment and love.

   _____ 2. It is wrong to arouse oneself sexually because it promotes an attitude of selfishness.

   _____ 3. Sexual intercourse is much more than just a biological function, more than just the release of tension.

   _____ 4. Honesty and respect for one another are absolutely essential in boy-girl relationships.

   _____ 5. To learn about love, sexual or not, one must know the meaning of self-control.

   Discuss: Why did you mark these statements as you did?

B. *Competing Values*: Many elements in our society influence the way we think about sexual morality. Here are some of them. Do the task assigned for each of the sources listed.

1. *The church.* The church bases its teaching about sexual morality on Jesus and his Father's revelation in both the Old and New Testament. The natural law also has an important part to play. Read the following scripture passages, then decide which of the statements in exercise A above St. Paul would agree with:

   1 Corinthians 6:12-20   Colossians 3:5-11

2. *Your parents.* Ask your parents how they would mark the items in exercise A. Ask them to give reasons for their choices. Share these in class.

3. *Your friends.* Ask your best friend to mark this same exercise.

4. *The media.* Find examples from the following media which go directly against the positive Christian values stated in exercise A.

Examples

- movies   _____

                    _____

- television programs _____

                    _____

- magazines   _____

                    _____

- song   _____

                    _____

- media "stars"   _____

                    _____

Discuss: Share your lists and discuss the values in each example.

1. To what extent are young people affected either consciously or unconsciously by the media?

2. Should parents censor what teen-agers see, read or listen to? Why or why not? If not, at what age is censorship no longer possible or even desirable?

SCRIPTURAL VIEWS OF SEX

Old Testament

Because God creates all things and looks on what he creates as being very good, we conclude that sex is also very good. In addition, because sex is such a powerful expression of love, and because God is love, human sexuality can be seen as a true sharing in the life of God. It is a great good through which humans participate in God's own creative activity.

A conclusion to these biblical insights is that sexual sins are not sins because sex is bad, but rather because it is so good. Sexual sins are a form of irresponsibility, a failure to acknowledge the depth of love implied in sexual relationships. Sexual organs, acts, feelings and thoughts, in themselves, can be nothing but good. We can deny our own sexuality only at the price of a self-destructive denial of our humanity.

We abuse our sexual powers when we use them contrary to the way God intends. The story of Adam and Eve, and the doctrine of original sin, show that the human heart easily becomes self-centered. Out of weakness we can use sex in a way that selfishly exploits our partner instead of acting in a context of committed love.

New Testament

It is interesting that Jesus rarely refers to sexual sins at all, and when he does it is in the context of forgiving them. This contrasts sharply with his frequent and sometimes severe condemnations of hypocrisy and pride.

There is certainly some validity in saying that the worst sins in Jesus' eyes are those committed in strength and not those committed out of the weakness of human nature. He condemned those who tried to make themselves morally superior to others.

Jesus calls for total inner renewal, turning from a self-centered to an other-centered life. Sexual sins, insofar as they flow from inner weakness, are not the focal point of Jesus' moral teaching. Jesus is most interested in the attitudes which flow from our hearts.

But the total conversion Jesus asks of us involves the whole person. It is a conversion of the inner attitudes which control our minds and our external actions. Jesus said:

> "You have learnt how it was said: *You must not commit adultery.* But I say this to you: if a man looks at a woman lustfully, he has already committed adultery with her in his heart" (Mt 5:27-28).

Jesus does not present a list of rules the Christian is not to break; rather, he calls for an attitude of love toward self and others. Within this attitude of responsible love, the abuse of sex is totally out of place. Scripture teaches that sexual sins are wrong, not because they are sexual, but because they are unloving and hence destructive uses of our sexual powers. Sexual sins are failures to love.

A REALISTIC VIEW OF HUMAN NATURE

The intent of this chapter has been to clarify the Christian attitude toward sex rather than to discuss specific questions of sexual morality in detail. Good judgment in issues of sexual morality calls for realistic acceptance of human nature enlightened by fidelity to the message of Jesus.

The following guidelines focus on a realistic acceptance of human nature.

1. God loves you and in his love you are called to love yourself. Failings in sexual morality are not occasions for self-hatred or belittlement; such attitudes are not true guilt but only neurotic self-destruction. We must be patient with ourselves and learn that a wholesome grasp of our sexuality comes with maturity and lifelong growth in Christ.

2. Many sins in the area of sexuality do not result from an isolated and deliberate act of the will. Rather, strong emotions, physical desires, deeply felt affection and other similar forces

often lessen our ability to make free and responsible choices. It is good to remember in such circumstances that the extent to which we do not have full control of the will is the extent to which blameworthiness for sin is lessened.

3. The pressures to go along with the crowd make it all the more difficult to maintain our moral integrity as Christians.

4. According to the gospel, not sexual sins but sins of unkindness, pride and hypocrisy most separate us from the love of God. We must avoid confusing an antisexual attitude with Christian morality.

The points above emphasize the importance of self-acceptance in evaluating sexual morality. The following points stress that a healthy acceptance of human nature means not simply accepting our weaknesses but also accepting our capacity to cooperate with the Lord's grace to live the way Jesus wants us to live.

1. Unkindness and pride are indeed among the most serious sins according to the gospel. But sexual sins are often expressions of unkindness and pride.

2. It is true that forces such as emotions can hinder free will and lessen our moral blameworthiness. By the same token, we must avoid those places and people that cause us to lose our freedom. Deliberately surrendering the ability to think clearly is itself a sign of insincerity and can bring with it moral guilt. Drinking, parking, attending drive-in movies, and petting are activities that a sincere person will regard with due caution. Human weakness is one thing; insincerity is another.

3. We should always remember that what may not cause temptation to one person may cause strong temptation to another. A mature, sincere couple will be honest with each other in this regard.

4. A good general rule to go by in trying to decide the morality of a sexual act is to ask yourself this question: Will this act make me (and my partner) more of a person before God, before myself, and before my loved ones?

5. Sex, wrongly used, can hurt others. Not only is this so in the obvious ways of venereal disease and unwanted pregnancy, but also in the broader context of a person's moral, psychological and social development.

6. There is no getting around the painful fact that to be Christian involves a willingness to be different from the crowd. The fact that "everyone is doing it" is not the issue. For Christians the issue is that sexual intercourse, and all acts directly leading to sexual intercourse, are reserved to the total commitment of married love. Sexual morality for the unmarried young adult is not founded on the idea that sex is bad; on the contrary, sex is a great good given to us by God both to share and grow in love and to help in God's plan for the transmission of life.

7. Catholics should always remember the help and strength that the Lord provides in the sacrament of reconciliation. He wishes to reassure the sinner of his Father's incredible love and to give spiritual strength to those who are struggling to live a Christian moral life.

TO DISCUSS

1. How are sexual actions different from other physical acts like walking, eating, talking, etc.?

2. How is Christian sexual morality both beautiful and difficult at the same time?

3. Should a boy resent it when a girl "draws the line" on a date? Should the girl resent it if the boy ignores her request? Should both the boy and girl share equally in the responsibility for setting limits on kissing and embracing? Where should the line be drawn on a date? Why?

4. Is it possible for two high school freshmen to be truly in love? two high school seniors?

5. Many people in our society claim that sexual intercourse is moral as long as the couple love each other. How would a Christian argue against this common opinion from the standpoint of the demands of the Lord?

SUMMARY

1. To be human is to be male or female. Human sexuality is rooted in our very being.

2. Sexuality is a basic component of all human relationships for it directly affects the way we give and receive love.

3. The church has always remained faithful to the biblical teachings on the goodness of human sexuality as created by God.

4. The goodness of human sexuality is revealed in its power to express a lifelong commitment to another in marriage and in the fact that through sexual intercourse new life is brought into existence.

5. In response to the Lord, the church teaches that sexual intercourse and all acts leading directly to it are moral only for married couples who have committed themselves to one another until death and have assumed responsibility for the children that might result from their union.

GOVERNMENT LAW

The newspapers remind us daily about the sexual practices of various age groups. They seem to delight in "telling all." One of the statistics cited time and time again is the number of people who engage in premarital sex. The message seems to be that it's OK if enough people are doing it.

Another item that receives considerable attention is whether parents have a right to know when their underage children get abortions or contraceptive devices.

What do you think?

Questions:

1. Do parents have the right to know if their underage child gets an abortion? Why or why not?

2. Do parents have the right to know if their underage child ob-
   tains a contraceptive device? Why or why not?

3. What are some possible consequences of keeping parents in
   the dark about their children's sexual practices?

4. Would you want to know if your teen-age children were
   engaging in premarital sexual intercourse? Why or why not?

5. If a friend told you he or she was involved in premarital sex,
   would you say or do anything? Why or why not? If you found
   out that a younger brother or sister was involved in
   premarital sexual intercourse, would you say or do
   anything? If so, what?

NINE
Respect for Life

The world's great religions all express awe and wonder at the mystery of life. Our religious sense calls forth a profound respect for life wherever it exists, from the smallest flower to humanity itself.

In some religions this respect goes to lengths which may seem strange to most of us. The followers of the Jain religion, for example, are reluctant to walk outdoors at night for fear of stepping on an insect and thus destroying life. Similarly, Buddhists strain their drinking water for fear of swallowing an insect.

Some religious groups are opposed to killing any higher life forms, especially animals; they are vegetarians because of their convictions. Likewise, they usually oppose all forms of violence directed against human beings, even in self-defense.

All of these religious practices flow from the deep conviction that life—all life—is sacred.

People of the Western world have generally followed the Jewish and Christian religions. The concept of life's sacredness is found frequently in both the Old Testament and the New Testament. Genesis boldly states that God created the whole universe and everything in it, and that God proclaimed the goodness of all that he had made. Furthermore, Genesis reveals that we humans hold a unique place in God's creation; we are made in his very image and likeness.

155

OLD TESTAMENT READINGS

1. As a class read Psalms 148 and 150. Discuss what they suggest our attitude toward nature should be. What are some implications of this attitude on environmental issues dealing with industrial pollution, atomic waste, forest preserves, strip mining, and so forth?

2. Read Psalm 121. What does it reveal about God's knowledge of and concern for each person he creates? How would this be important to anyone searching for a basis for respect for *all* people?

RESPECT FOR ALL PEOPLE

We all want to be respected by others. *Respect* means "to honor" or "to esteem" another. We quickly appreciate the importance of respect the moment we ourselves are laughed at, taken lightly, ignored, or in any way mistreated. Being the object of someone's disrespect is painful.

There are, however, different types of respect. The following exercise introduces several kinds.

KINDS OF RESPECT

Indicate on a scale of 1 to 5 the respect you have for each of the following. Let *1* represent very little respect; let *5* represent a great deal of respect.

1. a student council president

    ☐   ☐   ☐   ☐   ☐
    5   4   3   2   1

2. a star athlete

    ☐   ☐   ☐   ☐   ☐
    5   4   3   2   1

3. an "A" student

    ☐   ☐   ☐   ☐   ☐
    5   4   3   2   1

4. a "plays-no-favorites" teacher

☐   ☐   ☐   ☐   ☐
5   4   3   2   1

5. your best friend

☐   ☐   ☐   ☐   ☐
5   4   3   2   1

6. a beggar

☐   ☐   ☐   ☐   ☐
5   4   3   2   1

7. an enemy

☐   ☐   ☐   ☐   ☐
5   4   3   2   1

Discuss:

1. Why did you choose as you did? Share your responses with your classmates.
2. How do you define *respect*?
3. Whom do you respect the most? Why?

Respect for Leadership Positions

One kind of respect is illustrated by the first example in the exercise above. We have a natural tendency to respect those in leadership positions. Consider the pomp and ceremony which surround the English royal family, or the adulation crowds have for the pope when he tours other countries. These point to the great esteem people have for leaders. However, practically any incident in the life of a public figure finds its way into the news media, and scandals among our public officials quickly cause us to lose respect for them.

Respect for leaders is usually focused not so much on the person as on the power and influence the leadership position confers on the person.

Respect Based on Talents

Respect for star athletes or exceptional students is based on their talents. Gifted artists, students, cooks, athletes and the like gain our admiration because they do something better than the average person. This kind of respect is often wedded to the respect we give leaders because gifted people are often chosen to be the leaders in our communities. Respect based on talents, like the respect based on position, is directed not so much toward the person as toward the gifts he or she possesses.

Respect Based on Personal Qualities

Another kind of respect is based on recognition of a certain admirable quality in a person. We may respect a teacher for her unwavering fairness or an invalid neighbor for his cheerfulness.

Some people become widely known and respected because they exemplify certain qualities: Mother Teresa for her selflessness, Gandhi for his commitment to non-violent resistance, Martin Luther King, Jr., for his dedication to justice. These people—who may well become leaders—earn our respect more for what they are than for what they do.

Respect Based on Friendship

Another example from the exercise, the respect we have for a close friend, refers to a kind of respect, like respect based on personal qualities, that is qualitatively superior to respect based on position or personal abilities. We respect a friend regardless of position or talent; we respect a friend simply because he or she is a unique person with whom we are united in a mutual bond of love and affection. We respect our friends for being the persons they are. The more genuine the friendship, the more true this becomes.

SELECTIVE RESPECT

Respect for others based on their position or their talents is important. It is a sad thing when we lose respect for our leaders or for the gifted among us. More significant to our personal growth, however, is the respect we have for people we look to as models of certain good qualities or for our friends and the members of our family. What all these forms of respect share in common, though, is a tendency to be selective. They include some, but exclude others.

For example, while waiting in a crowd to get a glimpse of a passing celebrity, we are most likely unaware of the people in the crowd with us as individuals who also deserve our respect. Yet each one of them is important.

We quite naturally respect the ones we love. It also seems natural that strangers and people who injure us in some way do not deserve our respect. But what seems natural in the second case can lead to outright disrespect and even violation of the rights due every human person.

MORE ON RESPECT

Jobs. Most of us admire hardworking people. At the same time, certain professions or jobs carry an aura of prestige while others are looked on as second-rate.

Below is a partial listing of career choices. Do the following:

1. Rank the occupations from the one you admire the most (*1*) to the one you admire the least (*14*).

2. Share and discuss your responses as a class. Be sure to discuss these questions:

   • Do we tend to label people according to the work they do?

   • What are some implications of this kind of labeling?

____plumber	____secretary	____used-car dealer
____professional athlete	____high school teacher	____school custodian
____airline pilot	____garbage collector	____attorney
____airline hostess	____mortician	____politician
____nurse	____medical doctor	

CHRISTIANITY AND RESPECT FOR LIFE

Our Christian faith is based on the fact of the incarnation, that the Word of God became flesh and lived with us. Jesus showed us most dramatically that to be fully human is to be Godlike, because God has made himself like us in everything except sin. In Jesus Christ, God has firmly identified himself with our humanity. So strong is this union that Jesus told us that whatever we do to the least of our fellow humans we do to him.

The gospels repeatedly show Jesus challenging the superficial and inadequate notions people had about respect. He warned his Jewish opponents that security did not rest in observation of the finer points of the Law or their ideas of personal holiness. Rather, he challenged them to become like children and to stop judging others.

Jesus showed that prostitutes, tax collectors, the poor, the frightened, women, the outcasts, sinners of all kinds and various other "losers" are loved by his Father and hence deserving of our respect. Always condemning the sin and never the sinner, Jesus saw everyone as his brother or sister, a child of God called to union with him forever.

Perhaps Jesus' most dramatic example of profound respect for others was enacted on the cross. He even respected his tormenters, his executioners. He did not condemn them or resist their misguided efforts. He did not speak out in anger or bitterness. Instead, while hanging on the cross, he prayed, "Father, forgive them; they do not know what they are doing" (Lk 23:34).

As followers of Jesus, we must respect and love others as he did. We are called to respect everyone we meet because all people are our brothers and sisters in Christ Jesus. We are all children of the Father. One key aspect of the church's mission is to foster and witness to universal respect for all people. As God's people we must speak out and act against every instance of insensitivity and indignity performed against others.

RESPECT-FOR-LIFE SURVEY

Directions: Check the statements with which you agree.

_____ 1. Life is the most precious gift God has given to us.

_____ 2. The most serious moral problem today is abortion.

_____ 3. I could never kill another human being.

_____ 4. Hunting of animals for sport is wrong.

_____ 5. The building of nuclear weapons is an unspeakable crime against humanity.

_____ 6. The death penalty, even for criminals like murderers and rapists, is a kind of revenge and thus against the law of Christ.

_____ 7. There should be strict laws banning the possession of handguns.

_____ 8. The problem with using drugs for fun is that the person is ultimately endangering the quality of the life given to him or her by God.

Discuss:

a. Share your responses with your classmates. Did anybody check all eight statements?

b. Why did you choose as you did? Defend your answers.

c. As a class, rewrite each statement in a way that 75 percent of the class can agree with it.

Jesus' Teaching. The texts below show how Jesus acted toward certain people, or present his teaching on how we should act toward others. Gather into small groups. Each group should look up one or more of the texts. Draft a statement summarizing what each text reveals about how we should act today. When finished, share your research.

Matthew's gospel:	5:38-48	7:1-5	25:31-40
Luke's gospel:	15:11-32	23:32	23:39-43
Mark's gospel:	1:40-42	5:1-15	9:36-37

What the New Testament teaches about respect for others applies to our need to respect ourselves, too. Discuss some implications of knowing that we are worthwhile and deserving of respect because of God's love for us. Contrast this with society's message that we are only "respectable" if we hold positions of prestige or demonstrate certain skills.

SOME CONTEMPORARY CONCERNS
AND RESPECT FOR OTHERS

With the important insights treated above as background, we can now briefly turn to some specific applications of the Christian respect for self and others.

Abortion

We generally understand abortion as the direct killing of unborn human life.

People have abortions for many reasons. Some want to "solve" a problem and get rid of an unwanted pregnancy; others abort because of economic reasons, social embarrassment or a host of other personal reasons. Still others genuinely do not respect human life or refuse to see or admit that unborn babies are truly human. Some also argue that a woman has the right to do what she wants with her own body.

It is in the nature of living things to develop. We often refer to various natural cycles: seed to plant to flower to seed; caterpillar to chrysalis to butterfly; embryo to fetus to child to adult. Breaking into one of these cycles by an act of violence—such as abortion—clearly interferes with the natural course of events; it is a violation of the natural law.

Faith adds an important dimension to our appreciation of the utmost sacredness of human life. It tells us that human life is a sacred gift from God, a mystery that we do not fully understand or control. The unborn child is not fully developed, but neither is anyone else on earth. Each of us is at a different stage of growth and development on a journey toward final perfection. No one has the right to take the life of the unborn baby simply because he or she has barely started on the journey of life.

Our faith then, as well as the natural law imprinted on our hearts, tells us that abortion, the destruction of innocent human life, is one of the great moral tragedies of our day.

ABORTION ARGUMENTS

The following arguments are often used to justify abortions. Find prolife arguments to counteract them and discuss your responses in class.

1. A woman can do whatever she wishes with her own body.
2. Abortion is moral because it is legal.
3. True human life doesn't begin until birth.
4. Abortion should be allowed in cases of rape, or when the baby might be retarded or otherwise handicapped.
5. Neither the Catholic church, nor any other group, has a right to impose its beliefs on others.

Note: A good resource is *Abortion: The Silent Holocaust* by Father John Powell (Argus, 1981); another is *A Private Choice* by John T. Noonan (Free Press, 1979).

Suicide

Suicide means the taking of one's own life. Undoubtedly most people who commit suicide do so because they are so emotionally disturbed that they act impulsively, or their perception of reality is so distorted by their anguish or depression that their freedom of choice is severely limited.

Restriction of freedom lessens one's moral blameworthiness, of course. However, it is possible for people to commit suicide willingly and with knowledge of what they are doing. They may argue that suicide gives them control of their own lives and enables them to escape a condition of life which they judge intolerable.

Traditionally, Christianity has rejected suicide as a form of playing God. St. Thomas Aquinas, for example, argued that suicide is a crime of homicide against society, depriving it of one of its members. We are social beings who cannot take upon ourselves the destruction of the unique person that we are for others; if we do so, we withdraw from a community which gives us life. Through suicide, a person rejects God by rejecting God's great gift of life. In addition, suicide deeply hurts loved ones and discourages them in their own task of living.

Christians reject suicide because we see that life is a great gift of God, not some commodity that can be disposed of whenever we see fit.

SUICIDE?

Read the following cases and use the questions as a basis for class discussion.

Case #1: A 24-year-old man poured gasoline over himself and lit a match in front of the United Nations Building. He did so to protest the lack of social justice for the poor nations of the world. His death was very painful, but swift.

Did this person commit suicide? Explain your answer.

Case #2: Maximilian Kolbe volunteered to take the place of a family man who had been condemned to a starvation bunker by the Nazis. His offer was accepted, and Father Kolbe died in the bunker two weeks later.

Did Father Kolbe commit suicide?

Case #3: A close friend of yours has seemed depressed for some time. You know that her family situation is pretty bad, and that things have not been going well for her at school either. Last night she started talking about what it would be like to die.

What would you say? What would you do?

Note: Approximately 400,000 young people between the ages of 15 and 24 attempt suicide every year. Suicide is the third leading cause of death among adolescents in the United States, exceeded only by accidents and homicides.

Young people who are contemplating or planning suicide often talk to their friends about it.

Euthanasia

Many factors make euthanasia (mercy killing) a complex moral question. Technology today has produced machines, medicines and operations that can prolong life artificially almost indefinitely. This raises the complex question of when these extraordinary means can be morally withdrawn from a dying patient.

There are no easy answers. One thing is certain, though:

Under no circumstances can an individual directly take the life of another. Catholic morality cannot condone administering a chemical substance or performing a surgical procedure intended to kill a sick or dying patient.

Catholic morality does not require the use of *extraordinary* means to keep a person alive, however; a person does have the right to die in peace. Thus *not* performing a rarely used and expensive procedure on a hopelessly ill and dying patient is permitted if extreme caution is taken in order to make sure that life is respected. For example, the patient should be consulted if possible.

The classic Catholic statement on euthanasia comes from the writing of Pope Pius XII (1957). After stating that the natural law and Christian morality demand that we preserve our life and health, the pope wrote:

> But normally one is held to use only ordinary means—according to the circumstances of persons, places, times and cultures—that is to say, means that do not involve any grave burdens for oneself or another. A more strict obligation would be too burdensome for most men and would render the attainment of a higher, more important good too difficult. Life, health, all temporary activities are in fact subordinated to spiritual ends. On the other hand, one is not forbidden to take more than the strictly necessary steps to preserve life and health, as long as he does not fail in some more serious duty (*The Prolongation of Life*).

REFLECTION

Suppose that a local politician is proposing a bill that would allow euthanasia for the severely mentally handicapped, the hopelessly senile and others whom society might deem useless. Compose a letter to this politician in which you present arguments against the proposal.

War

The issue of war also touches on the problem of respect for life. Traditionally, the Catholic church has accepted the just-war theory which holds that a nation may morally engage in war as long as all of the following conditions are met:

1. The decision for war must be made by legitimate authority.

2. The war must be one of defense against unjust aggression.

3. War must be a last resort, when all other measures have failed.

4. There must be a good chance that the objectives for which the war is waged are achievable.

5. The good to be achieved by the war must outweigh any evil that will result from it. (For example, one cannot destroy a city in order to "save" it.) This is known as the *Principle of Proportionality*.

6. The principles of natural and international law must be adhered to. (For example, nothing can justify the indiscriminate killing of civilian populations.)

Although the just-war theory was developed out of a respect for human life, war of any kind challenges us with profound moral problems. The unbelievable power of nuclear weapons and their capacity to destroy our planet has caused the bishops of our country to condemn their use. The long, bitter struggle in Vietnam has also caused many Christians to question the validity of war in any form. Again, as with euthanasia, the issues are complex. War is always immoral, though, at the moment that those involved intentionally begin to ignore the dignity of human life.

Some examples of attacks against human dignity in war are the killing of noncombatants, the wounded, and the aged; the torturing of prisoners; and actions such as cutting off food and water supplies to entire cities causing civilian casualties.

War presents moral problems because it appears almost impossible to engage in war without also taking part in such activities.

Some Christians are called to witness against all war, paying the price of their convictions. We call them pacifists, those who object out of conscience to all war. The Christian pacifist can never stand up and demand that all who profess to be Christian must follow in his or her footsteps. But in light of Jesus' command to "love your enemies and pray for those who persecute you" (Mt 5:44), the pacifist is a constant reminder that war at best is a necessary evil. Human life flourishes where there is peace interiorly and in society at large. Jesus calls all his disciples to be peacemakers.

WAR

1. Obtain a copy of the American bishops' statement on the morality of war and nuclear weapons. Read it and make a report to the class.

2. Using the list of conditions for a just war, can nuclear war ever be justified? Discuss.

3. With so many people in the world starving to death, is it moral to use vast sums of money for more and more nuclear arms? Explain.

4. Some moralists argue that the issue of nuclear war dwarfs all other moral issues facing us today. Do you agree? Why or why not?

5. Research the causes of World War II. By the principles given, was it a just war? Explain.

Addiction

The toll taken by alcohol abuse on the quality of a person's life, as well as the lives of his or her family and the broader community, is staggering. Statistics show that ten million Americans are alcoholics, and that 25,000 people die each year in automobile accidents involving the abuse of alcohol.

A similar problem is physical or psychological addiction to a wide variety of chemical substances such as tranquilizers, marijuana and cocaine. Regardless of the substance used and its particular effects, such abuse is an attack on the quality of human life.

TO DISCUSS

1. Make a list of reasons young people use alcohol or drugs. Are there moral solutions to some of the problems presented? Are some of the reasons merely excuses to justify wrong behavior? If a person becomes an addict, what can he or she expect of the future? What will his or her life be like?

2. The Surgeon General has found a statistically significant correlation between smoking cigarettes and lung cancer. Few people doubt this correlation. Given the fact that lung cancer shortens life, is it immoral to smoke? Is it immoral to advertise cigarettes?

MAKING A CHOICE

The Christian ideal of respect for life is summarized in this quotation from the American bishops' pastoral letter, *Human Life in Our Day:*

> Christians believe God to be the "source of life" (Jn 5:26) and of love since "Love comes from God" (1 Jn 4:7). "God is love" (1 Jn 4:8) and man has been made "in his image and likeness" (Gn 1:26). Thus, man is most himself when he honors life and lives by love. Then he is most like God.

> In her defense of human life the Church in our day makes her own, as did Moses, the words in which God himself reduces our perplexities to a clear, inescapable choice:

> "I call heaven and earth to witness against you this day that I have set before you life and death . . . therefore, choose life that you and your descendants may live. . . ." (Dt 30:19).

As the above quotation suggests, respect for life remains little more than words unless we choose to put Christ's call to respect all life into practice daily. Such a choice is not easy. Prejudice, indifference, hurt feelings over past wrongs and other forces tend to limit us to a selective respect that excludes certain people or groups of people.

With prayer and a sincere desire to cooperate with God's grace, we can learn to respect ourselves and others in light of our awareness of God's love and concern for all of us, his children. By making this choice, and doing our best to carry it out daily, we can make a difference in the lives of "the least of these"—the neglected and hurting people in our world.

SUMMARY

1. Respect for others is important for our human growth and development.

2. Respect based on position, talents, personal qualities or feelings of love, however, tend to be selective; they include some while excluding others.

3. Jesus taught a message of universal love that excludes no one, even enemies. The Christlike love we should all practice flows from the Father's universal love for all his children regardless of their situation in life or their past failings. In our Lord Jesus Christ we are all united as brothers and sisters.

4. To put universal love into practice means to be concerned about and sensitive to every situation in which the happiness and well-being of anyone or any group is threatened. Christians will, for example, respect life by:

- speaking out for unborn babies
- rejecting suicide as an attack on God's precious gift of life
- refusing to treat sick and dying people as objects to be disposed of at will
- working actively for peace
- respecting their bodies by avoiding substances which may be addictive

PROJECTS

1. Research another world religion (for example, Judaism or Hinduism) to see what it teaches and practices in the area of respect for life.

2. Research in greater depth one of the respect-for-life topics treated in this chapter. Or consider the morality of one of the following:

- use of drugs in sports
- capital punishment
- building nuclear power plants
- paying farmers *not* to produce crops when many of the world's people are hungry.

CASE

It is generally acknowledged that the automobile industry and all the industries which support it are important for the strength of our economy.

In the past decade or so, though, foreign companies have provided stiff competition for the American automaker. As a result, a number of auto workers have been put out of work.

Some people suggest that if the American government did not impose such demanding quality control on the American auto industry—for example, in the areas of safety and pollution—American cars could be produced more cheaply and sold at a more competitive price. There is probably some truth in this charge.

Question: Should the standards imposed on American auto production be lowered? By doing so, more cars could be sold and more Americans would be put to work. However, air pollution would increase and there would be a greater risk of serious or even fatal injury to accident victims.

Discuss:

1. Where should the government draw the line in protecting the environment or the lives of the citizens?

2. Is it wrong to dismantle the pollution control devices on a car to get better gas mileage? Explain.

3. Is it wrong not to "buckle up" for safety? Explain.

TEN

The Community
Dimension in Morality

> *The whole group of believers was united, heart and soul; no one claimed for his own use anything that he had, as everything they owned was held in common.*
>
> *The apostles continued to testify to the resurrection of the Lord Jesus with great power, and they were all given great respect.*
>
> *None of their members was ever in want, as all those who owned land or houses would sell them, and bring the money from them, to present it to the apostles; it was then distributed to any members who might be in need.*
>
> —St. Luke

Word association games help to reveal our true thoughts on a given topic. This chapter deals with an elusive dimension in morality—the role of the Christian community. The exercise on the next page is designed to provoke a spontaneous response to certain concepts dealing with this topic.

WORD ASSOCIATION

As you see each word, jot down the first thought that comes to mind. For example, some people think of "authority" when they see the word *pope.* Honestly react to these words:

church _____

Jesus _____

Christian _____

morality _____

community _____

Catholic _____

Gather into groups of three to five and compare responses. How many of your initial reactions were people-centered? How many were oriented to institutions? Do any of them leave you with warm feelings—like acceptance, peace, joy, forgiveness? Do any leave you feeling cold? Can you see a common theme uniting them all?

MORALITY AND COMMUNITY

Earlier in the book we saw that morality by definition includes the concept of community. Morality tries to discover the norms of human conduct in light of revelation. We have seen that Christians believe that all people are children of God, each with unique worth and tremendous dignity. We are brothers and sisters in and through Jesus Christ by the power of the Holy Spirit. Hence, our moral response to God involves a community dimension.

Another view defines morality as *our response to the demands that others place on us.* In this view of Christian morality, others are involved at the very core of our living a moral life. We are moral to the degree that we respond to those who call on us, who ask us for love, who ask us to respond to them and their human needs in some way. Our responding to others in community determines how well we are living as children of God. This concept is certainly compatible with Jesus' teaching to love even the unlovable, even our enemies.

A third way to look at the community dimension in morality is to read and prayerfully reflect on 1 Corinthians 12:12–3:13. In this important text St. Paul emphasizes that the Spirit of Jesus and his Father unites us into one body. We are intimately related to one another; each member needs the others in order that the body be whole. If a single member suffers, the entire body is affected. In other words, because we have been created as a unit—a community—by the power of God's love, our response to God is always going to involve others. The heart of Christian morality is that it is communal.

WHY LIVE A CHRISTIAN MORAL LIFE?

These definitions of morality are, of course, Christian definitions of morality. But this question may have occurred to you: Why should I live a Christian moral life?

This is an excellent question, certainly in light of the fact that there are many other good people in the world besides Christians. For example, suppose a young man ran into the street and sacrificed his life to save a young child from an oncoming car. Would it make any difference whether he was Catholic or atheist?

In one sense, it might make no difference at all. In either case a young child's life was saved.

But in another sense, it could make a difference. The Christian might be acting out of his fundamental belief that the greatest love he can show others is to sacrifice his life for them—and thus be witnessing to the presence of the Lord Jesus Christ in our midst. His action could lead others to God and to the hope of eternal life.

Living a Christian moral life serves as a beacon of light to others who are searching for meaning in life. When people see genuine love they ask: "What motivates you? Why are you living this way when it is so easy to use others and think only of yourself?" This is precisely what happened in the early church. People were drawn to the Lord because they saw his love in action.

If you follow Jesus and respond to him in love, you will also be attracting others to the Lord. You will witness to the fact that Jesus lives today. You will provide people the hope that they are looking for—that we are all destined to a supernatural life in union with our Father in heaven.

CHRISTIAN WITNESSING

Very few of us are called to surrender our lives for the Lord. But daily we are called on to die to ourselves and thus witness to him. What kind of witness are you?

Here are some situations in which you might find yourself. Choose your most likely response from the options given.

_____ 1. I am in the presence of someone who is using our Lord's name in vain.

   I would . . .

   a. gently tell the person to improve his or her language

   b. probably not do anything because it is not that big a thing

   c. I don't know what I'd do

   d. other: _____

_____ 2. I have just finished reading a book about the seriousness of the nuclear arms race.

   I would . . .

   a. join some kind of peace movement

   b. tell someone about the book and some of the things I learned

   c. do nothing

   d. other: _____

_____ 3. Half the class is cheating on an exam.

I would . . .

  a. not cheat and report the cheaters

  b. not cheat and mind my own business

  c. join in the cheating

  d. other: _____

_____ 4. A friend is rapidly becoming an alcoholic.

I would . . .

  a. tell her parents so she will get professional help

  b. try to talk her out of drinking

  c. probably do nothing for fear that I might ruin our friendship

  d. other: _____

_____ 5. Some friends are gossiping about the sex life of one of my classmates.

I would . . .

  a. try to change the subject

  b. do nothing

  c. join in the fun

  d. other: _____

_____ 6. The parish priest asks for volunteers to give a witness talk at the next youth renewal.

I would . . .

  a. volunteer

  b. come up with an excuse

  c. pretend I didn't hear

  d. other: _____

Discuss:

1. Share responses. How many of your responses witness to a Christian value?

2. What is the hardest thing for you to do in regard to peer pressure? Why is it so hard? By resisting peer pressure, how might you be witnessing to the Lord Jesus?

3. Why is Christian love sometimes described as dying to self?
    How might some of the responses given above be con-
    sidered a death to self?

Part of the Lord's good news is that he wants everyone to
be saved. The Second Vatican Council spoke to this topic:

> Those also can attain to everlasting salvation who
> through no fault of their own do not know the gospel
> of Christ or His Church, yet sincerely seek God, and,
> moved by grace, strive by their deeds to do His will as
> it is known to them through the dictates of con-
> science. Nor does divine Providence deny the help
> necessary for salvation to those who, without blame
> on their part, have not yet arrived at an explicit
> knowledge of God, but who strive to live a good life,
> thanks to His grace. Whatever goodness or truth is
> found among them is looked upon by the Church as a
> preparation for the gospel. She regards such qualities
> as given by Him who enlightens all men so that they
> may finally have life (*Dogmatic Constitution on the
> Church*, No. 16).

If the above paragraph is true, then why be Christian? Why
live our lives under the banner of Jesus Christ?

Let us attempt to answer that important question. To be a
Christian is both a privilege and a challenge. By gratefully accepting the privilege and eagerly living out the challenge,
following Jesus can and does make a difference.

Being a Christian is a privilege in the sense that we have
been given an explicit awareness of God's total self-com-
munication to us—in the person of his Son, Jesus Christ. This
faith is a gift. God has chosen us because he has a task for
us to perform. The fact that he has chosen us does not make us
better than anyone else; it does, however, give us special
responsibilities.

The privileged knowledge we have of Jesus Christ gives us
hope, hope that the human condition is ultimately redeemable.
Our community of believers knows in faith that the evils, the
frustrations, the hates of this world will eventually pass away,

that they have been overcome by the suffering, death and resurrection of our Savior, Jesus Christ.

Our community of believers, the church which is the Body of Christ, has it on the word of our Lord that death is not the end. Jesus' sacrifice for us powerfully proclaimed that death is but a transition to a glorious new life. Our hope in a wonderful life of union with God and our friends makes life more meaningful.

But this privileged knowledge carries a challenge with it. We are not given our knowledge of Jesus just to keep him to ourselves and rest satisfied that we are saved. Rather, we are challenged by Jesus himself to go out into the world and preach in word and deed the good news of our redemption.

We must be Jesus people. As members of Christ's body, we must be his hands, his feet, his caring and sharing in the world today. In a real way, Jesus needs us, his church, to do his continuing work of healing and loving. To love as Jesus did is a challenge, a great responsibility entrusted to us.

We are also resurrection people. Our Christian living should point in a joyous and glad way to the ultimate victory of goodness and our eventual union with God our Father.

The Call to Service

Three images sum up the duty we have as Christians who have been blessed with the gift of faith. All three demand that we accept the challenge of Jesus Christ. All three teach us that to live as Christians means to offer the world what no other religion can.

Leaven. Jesus spoke of the kingdom of God using the image of leaven (yeast). The yeast pervades the dough and causes it to rise. The role of Christians in the world is to change it, to raise its awareness to the real meaning in life. The image of yeast does not put an emphasis on numbers or on quantity. It stresses quality. By the quality of our lives lived in response to God and others, we help through word and deed to show others who they are and what their destiny is.

Yeast exercises its power simply by being present in the dough. You, too, can exercise your power of witness simply by being at school, at play, at work, at home. Your presence can help bring the Lord into your world. Every minute of every day gives you a chance to show others around you what it means to be at peace and in love with the Lord Jesus Christ.

REFLECTION

Think of a way you can share the Lord's love right now. Resolve to help someone to experience God's love.

Light. Jesus called his followers to be the light of the world. Jesus is the true guiding light, and we have the task of letting his light reflect off us. We help others discover meaning in life by letting Christ and his life shine forth in the way we live.

In John's gospel, truth and light are often linked. When we tell the truth, we are allowing the Truth to shine through us. In a world which too often lies and deceives, the truth-teller is a shining example of God's presence in the world.

REFLECTION

Is it difficult for you to tell the truth? Why or why not? Jesus said, "The truth will make you free" (Jn 8:32). Tell the class about a time this happened to you.

Salt. Jesus also called his followers to be the salt of the earth. This image carries several meanings. First, salt is a preservative. In the days before freezers, meat was "salted down" to keep it from spoiling. Second, salt is a flavoring, a seasoning. Imagine eating a sweet and juicy ear of corn without a dash of salt. A sprinkling of salt can make all the difference in the world.

You are salt, too. You can make all the difference in the

world. By living a Christian life, you can change the world. Your deeds help bring Jesus' saving touch into the world today. You participate in his work of salvation.

Today, more than ever, Christian witness is needed in the area of social justice. We are called to act on behalf of the poor, the downtrodden, not out of charity, but out of justice.

But let justice flow like water,
and integrity like an unfailing stream (Am 5:24).

If we don't, then we are tasteless, and no one is going to pay attention to us or our message that God is love. We show people that God is love when we love the needy in our midst.

WORKING FOR JUSTICE

Christians must witness to the truth of Jesus and his message by showing concern for the needy. Here are three moral problems which concern needy people. Discuss what you as an individual and as a member of a Christian community can do about each.

1. A classmate is lonely, scared, and in desperate need of a friend.

2. As you read this, there are people in your town applying to a hunger center for food. They are unemployed and dejected.

3. There are several nursing homes in your community. As you read this, an old lady is sitting beside her bed with no one to visit her. She'd love to have someone read to her.

Challenge: As a class, devise a service project to help "do justice" to one of the situations described above.

Why be a Christian? Why live a Christian moral life? The answers lie in our willingness to participate in spreading the good news of Jesus. It is a challenge to live our lives as Christians, but it is a challenge—when lived—which helps the rest of humanity to know that there is a God, a God who cares for us very much and wants us to be reunited with him in eternity. By joyfully living as Jesus would have us live we make believable the claim that we are saved and that God has wondrous things in store for us and for all our brothers and sisters.

MEETING JESUS AS A CATHOLIC

Most of you who are reading this book are Christians who belong to a particular community, the Catholic church. As Catholics, we believe that Jesus gave the church the authority, and the duty, to teach in the areas of faith and morals. This authority resides in the *magisterium* of the church, that is, in the bishops with the pope as their head.

What should our attitude be toward the teachings of our bishops and the pope? Certainly we have a serious obligation to form our consciences in light of them. We should, for example, weigh very seriously all the non-infallible teachings of the magisterium and accept in faith all the infallible teachings of our pope. As a Catholic community we believe that these teachings are guided by the Holy Spirit. We believe Jesus' promise to remain with his church and guide it on its journey through time.

As Catholics, then, we have a great help in learning to do the right thing: the teaching authority of the church. A second great help in doing the right thing is the presence of Jesus in his church. Jesus is really and totally present to his people in his church and also in each Christian who allows the Lord to live in him or her.

Further, our Lord is present in the sacraments. This presence is powerfully demonstrated in the Eucharist, the key sacrament to which all the others build.

The Eucharist is often called a celebration because through this sacrament we celebrate who we are in union with our Lord.

The Eucharist celebrates our being with others who believe as we do. Our coming together at Mass is quite special because we do it to worship God the Father and to recognize that we, as Christians, go to the Father with one another guided by Jesus, our brother.

Communal worship is psychologically sound. Because we are social beings, we need the support and help of our fellow believers. We need the nourishment of our Lord in holy communion. We live in a society that thinks many of our Christian values are insane. As a result, it is very difficult to follow the Lord and live a moral, Christian life. We need his help and the help of our brothers and sisters. Liturgy is a special time to remember our vocation and our promised destiny. It is a time to remember that we need the help of God's Son to live out our vocation with others.

Going to Mass is also an opportunity to show love to everyone assembled. At times we might prefer not to go to Mass. But by going and participating and worshiping with our brothers and sisters we make a strong statement: "I value you and the Lord. I am here to share myself with you."

The Eucharist nourishes the Catholic by means of God's word. We derive nourishment not only from the Word—the Son—when we receive him in holy communion, but we derive nourishment from the written word which is proclaimed at Mass. The word of God proclaimed, thought about and prayed over becomes a living Word that helps us become who we are. As sons and daughters of the Father we need constant reminders of our dignity. The liturgy of the Mass strengthens our community to live out the implications of who we are.

The Eucharist is a symbol, a sign, for others, especially visible when we gather on the Lord's day. We celebrate on the first day of the week to commemorate the day our Lord was raised from the dead. The Eucharist is a community sign of unity and serves as an example of light and hope. It also proclaims to the world that there is an ultimate meaning to our existence. We are destined for a resurrected, eternal life in the Lord.

Morality, like the Eucharist, has much to do with community. We live out our lives with others. Christians today are in the same situation as the early church. We very much need one another and our Lord to help make it possible for us to live lovingly toward others. By experiencing the love of God in Christian community—and this is done in a unique way at the

Eucharist—we can better share this love with others not only in our own Christian community, but outside it as well.

EUCHARIST

1. List the five most common reasons for going to Mass on Sunday. Make another list of the five most common reasons people don't go.

   Reasons people go

   a. _____

   b. _____

   c. _____

   d. _____

   e. _____

   Reasons people stay away

   a. _____

   b. _____

   c. _____

   d. _____

   e. _____

   Which statement most accurately reflects your own attitude?

   Discuss: What does the Eucharist mean to you? Has the Lord ever helped you in a special way through this sacrament? Explain.

2. A friend comes to you and says that she has stopped going to Sunday liturgy at her parish because she doesn't get anything out of it. How would you help her see that it is not what we get out of it but rather what we put into it that really matters?

SUMMARY

1. Christian morality by definition involves others; because we are members of Christ's body, we are intimately related to one another.

2. One reason for living a Christian moral life is to *witness* to the good news of God's love in Jesus Christ. This love is for everyone; thus, it is possible for everyone to attain salvation.

3. Being a Christian is both a privilege and a challenge. It is a privilege because we know that we are redeemed by the Lord and are destined for eternal life. In faith we know that life has meaning. It is a challenge because we must live joyfully and lovingly toward others, sharing in word and deed the special relationship with the Lord we have been privileged to experience.

4. Christians have the responsibility to be "leaven, light and salt":

   a. *leaven* which raises the consciousness of the people to God's saving acts in Jesus Christ;

   b. *light* which allows the truth to shine forth to all;

   c. *salt* which saves the world and gives it a different flavor.

5. Christian moral life demands that we should be passionately concerned with the poor, the weak, "the least of these."

6. Catholics believe that Jesus continues to teach to his church through the bishops and the pope, the magisterium. Magisterial teaching in the area of morals helps form the Catholic conscience on moral issues.

7. Catholics believe in the sacramental presence of Jesus. We believe that especially in the Eucharist the Lord comes to us as individuals and as a community to give us the strength to live the kind of life he requires of us.

CHRISTIAN WITNESS—FAITH INTO ACTION

1. Clip 10 articles from your local newspaper that depict current social problems in your community.

2. Choose one that you think *you* can do something about.

3. List four things that could help solve this problem.

4. Choose one thing from this list of four which you think you can do effectively.

5. List things that will help you accomplish your task. Make another list of things that might hinder you.

6. Do something about the social problem you chose.

   or

   Discuss the clippings in class. Select one which everyone agrees is a moral issue that merits our concern as Christians. What can you do as individuals about it? as a class? as a parish community?

7. Discuss your project with your classmates.

ELEVEN

Christian Morality— Summary and Problems

Morality does not make a Christian, yet no man can be a Christian without it.
—Daniel Wilson

This chapter summarizes some of the main themes of this book. It ends with several moral problems or situations which ask you to apply what you have learned.

SUMMARY OF THEMES

1. Our philosophy of the human person often determines how we act toward others. Various views of the human person, some of which are definitely not Christian, bombard us in our daily lives. Our pluralistic society speaks with many voices. Those calling us to recognize human dignity for all should be heeded; those calling us to evil must be disregarded, in fact, spoken out against.

2. Some of the philosophies of life promoted in today's world create an atmosphere in which it is difficult for people to find God or even to see that God is worth asking about at all. These attitudes contribute to some of the great moral tragedies of our day: abortion, euthanasia, the arms race, poverty, sexual promiscuity, prejudice against the weak and defenseless.

3. Both the natural law and divine revelation help Christians see that we should have a refreshingly optimistic view about human nature. Christianity maintains that each person is fundamentally good, redeemable and loved by God. It holds that each person, whether the person knows it or not, is a child of God and brother or sister to Jesus Christ and to every other person.

187

4. A basic principle of Christian morality is that each person ought to have attitudes and perform actions that are in harmony with the dignity of his or her own nature. This human dignity includes not only our role as children of the Father, but also the dignity to think and choose. It involves the ability to love. It includes individual uniqueness lived in social contact. It holds that we are God's image and his co-partner in the development of creation.

5. Christian morality can be described as a free response to the love relationship we have with all others as brothers and sisters in Christ. As creatures endowed with a certain degree of freedom, we are responsible for our freedom. We are called to respond in love to the demands our brothers and sisters place on us. Because we are intimately related to Jesus Christ, we show our love of God by responding to the Lord's teachings under the guidance of the Holy Spirit.

6. The message of Jesus is summed up in the word *love.* Christian love consists of an active concern for others. It involves trusting in God and willingly serving others. It requires doing more than the expected. It involves forgiveness. It means a willingness to suffer. It means prayer and good works done in a spirit of humility. It demands holding the world's goods in perspective—using them, but not becoming their slave.

7. Conscience is the ability to judge the rightness or wrongness of our actions and attitudes. When properly formed and followed, conscience helps us become the person Jesus Christ intends us to be. Our duty is twofold: We must develop our conscience continuously; we must follow the dictates of our conscience. Among other things, a Christian conscience manifests purity of intention, evidence of consulting the teaching of Jesus and his church, and a prayerful openness to the action of the Holy Spirit.

8. Laws are objective guidelines to help us control our external actions for the sake of the inner freedom to be all we can possibly be. Natural law is universally knowable by all people. Civil law is each society's particular interpretation and application of the natural law. Divine law is known in faith; it comes from God in revelation. Church law is the particular application for the Christian community of divine law.

9. Divine law is best understood as a covenant relationship between us and God. Covenant is an open-ended, totally committed love. In all love relationships we are free to do what we have to do in order to be true to love. Thus laws are important for Christians, but only because faithfulness to love is important. Laws do not save us. Only Jesus, the Son of God, saves us.

10. Sin is an alienation from a living relationship with God and others. It always has social implications. It often flows from basic attitudes of pride and self-centeredness, and shows itself in actions as well as in failures to act. We are morally guilty of sin if the action we perform or the attitude we hold is contrary to God's law and if knowledge of wrongdoing and consent of the will are present.

11. Christians believe that through the saving power of Jesus Christ sin is forgiven and its ultimate effect, death, has been overcome. Catholics believe they can encounter in a special way the forgiving, healing touch of Jesus in the sacrament of reconciliation.

12. Sex, as created by God, and as an expression of love and the means of bringing about new life, is essentially good. Sexual sins abuse the goodness of sex by using it irresponsibly, by a failure to love according to God's will as made known to us in revelation.

13. Christian sexual morality calls on us to form proper attitudes about human sexuality and to seek the highest possible ideals. At the same time we must accept our human weakness. We must distinguish between sexual sins committed out of weakness and sins committed deliberately to hurt or degrade ourselves or others, or in open indifference to our relationship to God. We must also remember our Lord stands ready to give us his strength and grace to enable us to live as he wants us to live.

14. We naturally tend to respect loved ones. But Christians are called to respond to the basic dignity of others in light of God's love which embraces all people everywhere. Respect for the lives of others must extend even to our enemies.

15. Living a life of Christian morality in the Catholic tradition is done in community. Morality is, in brief, a loving response to the demands that others place on us. We need the strength and help of the church to do what the Lord requires of us. Our presence should and does make a difference. We are the light of the world, leaven and salt of the earth. We celebrate our Christian vocation in the Eucharist, the great sacrament of Christian unity.

MORAL PROBLEMS FOR ANALYSIS

Here are some cases to test your understanding of the principles of Christian morality. The solutions are rarely simple. Christians must use their God-given intelligence to discern his will in the world.

Try to apply the moral principles presented in this book by asking questions like these:

- What is the teaching of Jesus?

- What does the church say about this topic?

- What are the alternatives? consequences?

- Does this add to human dignity or subtract from it?

- Is this consistent with being a child of God?

- What role do law and personal conscience play here?

- Is this loving?

(As a class, add at least three more questions to this list.)

- _____

- _____

- _____

PROBLEM #1: The Term Paper

Joan is a junior in high school. She works part time to help her mother with the expenses of raising the family. Her father is deceased. Joan is a good student who does not fear hard work. She is taking a difficult chemistry course this semester. Her teacher is one of the toughest in the school.

During the semester, the teacher assigns two 10-page term papers. In simple terms, Joan does not have the time to write one of the papers. Science is not her academic strength, nor does her planned career demand that she have an extensive knowledge of science.

A classmate offers to do her paper in exchange for $20. The friend is a science whiz and is sure to do an "A" job. Joan is seriously considering taking her up on the offer.

Discuss:

1. What would you advise Joan to do? Why?

2. List some reasons for and against her proposed action.

3. What would *you* do in the circumstances?

PROBLEM #2: Taxes

Gary has just finished a course in Christian morality. He has studied the Sermon on the Mount and is convinced that war is immoral. He believes that the nuclear arms race is a blatant affront to God and his creation.

Gary has decided to take a stand on this issue. Through several part-time jobs this past year, he has earned $3,500. No federal income tax was withheld from his paychecks because of the nature of his jobs. Now, at income tax time, he realizes that he owes the federal government some money. He realizes that a sizable percentage of the federal tax goes to the military. As a result, he is seriously considering paying only that portion of the tax which will be used for nonmilitary purposes.

Discuss:

1. Based on Christian principles, what should Gary do?

2. What would *you* do? Why?

3. Do Christians have an obligation to protest immoral actions of their government? Explain.

PROBLEM #3: Picketing

You are caught in a dilemma. Your parish priest has asked you and other members of the parish youth group to picket an "adult bookstore" which carries pornographic reading materials and "art" movies. The bookstore has moved into the business district of your town. It strictly limits its visitors to those 21 years of age and older. A person has to show an I.D. to gain entrance to the store.

You have been reading about censorship and individual freedoms. Your general feeling is against censorship. But your parish priest—a good and wise man—is exerting pressure to close the store and is enlisting your aid.

Discuss:

1. What would you do? Why?

2. What should be done in this case and cases like it?

3. Are there any good reasons not to close this store? Explain.

PROBLEM #4: Birth Control Pills

This case unfortunately involves you.

You happen to be rummaging through your 16-year-old sister's belongings for the sweater she borrowed from you last week when you come across some birth control pills. The prescription is in her name.

Directions: Think of three possible courses of action. List several consequences for each action.

Alternative #1: _____

    Consequence a: _____

    Consequence b: _____

    Consequence c: _____

Alternative #2: _____

    Consequence a: _____

    Consequence b: _____

    Consequence c: _____

Alternative #3: _____

    Consequence a: _____

    Consequence b: _____

    Consequence c: _____

What would you do? What should you do?

PROBLEM #5: Linda[1]

Linda failed to return home from a dance Friday night. On Saturday she admitted she had spent the night with an Air Force lieutenant.

Her parents decided on a punishment that would "wake Linda up." They ordered her to shoot the dog she had owned for about two years.

On Sunday, the parents and Linda drove the dog into the desert near their home. They had the girl dig a shallow grave. Then her mother grasped the dog's head between her hands and her father gave his daughter a .22 caliber pistol and told her to shoot the dog.

Instead, the girl put the pistol to her right temple and shot herself. The police said there were no charges that could be filed against the parents except possibly cruelty to animals.

On the basis of Christian morality, what immoral act (if any) was committed by each person involved?

1. Linda

2. The lieutenant

3. Her parents

4. The police

Discuss: Which of the actions involved appears to most seriously disrupt the love relationship with God and with others?

---

1. This story is quoted from Jeffry Schrank's *Teaching Human Beings: 101 Subversive Activities for the Classroom* (Boston: Beacon Press, 1972, pp. 66-68). Schrank excerpted it from *Search for a New Land,* by Julius Lester (New York: Dial Press, 1968).

PROBLEM #6: The Letter

Suppose you write an advice column for your diocesan newspaper. One day you receive the following letter:

Dear Moralist,

I know I am asking you to play God, but I desperately need your help.

My grandfather, 65 years old, is very ill. Unless he receives a kidney, he has only a short time to live. The doctors have told my family, though, that Gramps has an excellent chance to live for many more years if he receives a healthy kidney from a family donor.

Should I donate my kidney? I'm afraid of this operation and what it will do to my own life span. But I'll never forgive myself if Gramps dies.

What should I do?

Write your response here:

PROBLEM #7: The Judge

A Catholic judge has just presided over a murder case. The jury found the defendant guilty and recommended the maximum penalty.

The state allows capital punishment (in this case, the electric chair) in order to deter other potential criminals. There is tremendous popular support for the death penalty in this case.

However, the judge believes, in conscience, that capital punishment is just a sophisticated form of revenge.

Discuss:

1. What should the judge do? Why?

2. Suppose the judge decides for life imprisonment, rather than for the death penalty. Would *not* enforcing the state law permitting capital punishment be acting immorally?

3. Does a public official have an obligation to set aside his or her personal conscience when called on to fulfill a sworn duty to uphold the laws of the land? Explain.

PROBLEM #8: Theft or Not?

Is taking things like soap, ashtrays and towels from a motel room wrong? These things are small and aren't worth much. In fact, some people claim that the cost is built into the amount charged for the rental of the motel room.

What do you say?

PROBLEM #9: Junk Food

Roughly two-thirds of the world goes to bed hungry each night.

In light of this frightening statistic, is it wrong for Christians to spend their money on and consume junk food?

What do you say?

PROBLEM #10: The Crying Baby

One of the most popular TV programs ever to hit the airwaves was M*A*S*H. Its last episode drew a tremendous viewing audience. But this last episode also provided an interesting moral dilemma. Here it is:

> Hawkeye—one of the doctor/heroes of the show—was on a bus with some fellow surgeons and a few Koreans. He informed the driver of the bus that some enemy soldiers were approaching, and the bus should be hidden by the side of the road.
>
> As the enemy soldiers were walking by the bus, an infant in the bus began to cry.

What should the mother do in this situation? Should she muffle the baby (with the real risk the baby will suffocate) to keep the occupants of the bus from being discovered? Or should she allow the baby to breathe (and cry) and thus risk discovery and possible death for all the people on the bus?

Discuss:

1. What should the mother do?

2. What would *you* do?

3. What would Jesus want us to do?

4. Are many lives worth more than one life?